AF582598

A TRIBUTE TO ANDHRA GRANTHALAYAM BIOGRAPHY OF MUCHUKOTA VENKATARAMAIAH

ANDHRA GRANTHALAYAM
1-8-1923 to 30-6-1979

MUCHUKOTA VENKATARAMAIAH
5-10-1894 to 4-4-1972

Copyright © Muchukotavenkataramaiah Chandrasekhar
All Rights Reserved.

This book has been self-published with all reasonable efforts taken to make the material error-free by the author. No part of this book shall be used, reproduced in any manner whatsoever without written permission from the author, except in the case of brief quotations embodied in critical articles and reviews.

The Author of this book is solely responsible and liable for its content including but not limited to the views, representations, descriptions, statements, information, opinions and references ["Content"]. The Content of this book shall not constitute or be construed or deemed to reflect the opinion or expression of the Publisher or Editor. Neither the Publisher nor Editor endorse or approve the Content of this book or guarantee the reliability, accuracy or completeness of the Content published herein and do not make any representations or warranties of any kind, express or implied, including but not limited to the implied warranties of merchantability, fitness for a particular purpose. The Publisher and Editor shall not be liable whatsoever for any errors, omissions, whether such errors or omissions result from negligence, accident, or any other cause or claims for loss or damages of any kind, including without limitation, indirect or consequential loss or damage arising out of use, inability to use, or about the reliability, accuracy or sufficiency of the information contained in this book.

Made with ♥ on the Notion Press Platform
www.notionpress.com

Sharing life with husband who considers himself to be the servant of humanity is a stupendous task.

This book is dedicated to My Mothers PARVATHAMMA and LAKSHMIDEVAMMA who followed their husband with all devotion and faced difficulties with a Smile.

M.V.R. CHANDRA SEKHAR

AUTHOR'S NOTE

Nothing is permanent in this world. Everything is apt to change with time.

Leaders and volunteers of Independence Movement sacrificed comforts, wealth, family life and their future for the sake of the country. They never craved for recognition. Family members also suffered untold miseries. Family members, well wishers in most cases did not record the sufferings undergone and sacrifices made by freedom fighters. Most of the records, memories vanished with time.

I wrote and published book in Telugu on my Father's Biography and Andhra Granthalayam with the Title "గ్రంథాలయ తాతయ్య" during the Year 2012, and another Book in English **A TRIBUTE TO ANDHRA GRANTHALAYAM - BIOGRAPHY OF MUCHUKOTA VENKATARAMAIAH** Copies of 99% of books are distributed free of cost in memory of my father. Publication of this book has also a reference to **75 Years of Indipendence Bharatha Swatanthra Swarna Mahotsava Celebrations.** Muchukota Venkataramaiah was the personification of Mahatma's definition of a volunteer.

I tried to present my father's devotion to service in this book as I felt it to be my duty. The book is delayed by three decades because of my ignorance.

Most of the information is collected from 1) Sarvothama Bhavan Library, Vijayawada. 2) Saraswatha Nikethanam library, Vetapalem, Prakasam Dist., 3) Krishna Devaraya Andhra Bhashanilayam, Hyderabad. The author is grateful to the authorities of the libraries for permitting me to collect relevant information.

Andhra Granthalayam Kurnool did similar service and was unique as it was an individual's effort. I also salute many friends and well wishers who are responsible for improvements made in this book.

I express my deep sense of gratitude to Dr. K. Sivabhushanam and N. Sreedhara Murthy who helped me at all stages in preparation of this book. Anchala Ravindranath helped me in procurement of relevant documents. Prof. Kumaraswamy Raju and K. Ramachandrarao scrutinised the book in the initial stages and suggested improvements. I am grateful to them.

M.V.R.Chandrasekhar

CONTENTS

	FORE WORD	P.No. 5
CHAPTER - 1	INTRODUCTION	P.No. 8
CHAPTER - 2	HISTORY AND STATUS OF EDUCATION IN THE FIRST DECADE OF TWENTIETH CENTURY	P.No. 17
CHAPTER - 3	ROLE OF VOLUNTEERS IN PEOPLE'S MOVEMENT	P.No. 19
CHAPTER - 4	LIBRARY MOVEMENT	P.No. 21
CHAPTER - 5	ANCESTORS OF VENKATARAMAIAH	P.No. 27
CHAPTER - 6	EDUCATION AND HOBBIES OF VENKATARAMAIAH	P.No. 30
CHAPTER - 7	KARMBHOOMI OF VENKATARAMAIAH	P.No. 35
CHAPTER - 8	REASONS FOR SHIFTING TO KURNOOL	P.No. 37
CHAPTER - 9	ANDHRA GRANTHALAYAM AT KOTHAPETA, KURNOOL FROM I923 TO 1935	P.No. 40
CHAPTER - 10	ANDHRA GRANTHALAYAMAT NARASIMHARAOPET	P.No. 47
CHAPTER - 11	VENKATARAMAIAH TEACHER - COLES MEMORIALHIGH SCHOOL, KURNOOL	P.No. 59
CHAPTER - 12	VENKATARAMAIAH AFTER RETIREMENT	P.No. 65
CHAPTER - 13	PARADOXES IN LIBRARY MOVEMENT	P.No. 69
CHAPTER - 14	TRIBUTES FOR SERVICES RENDERED TO LIBRARY MOVEMENT	P.No. 72
CHAPTER - 15	DEMISE OF VENKATARAMAIAH	P.No. 77
CHAPTER - 16	CONCLUSION	P.No. 80
	ANNEXURE - 1	P.No. 82
	ANNEXURE - 2	P.No. 83
	ANNEXURE - 3A	P.No. 85
	ANNEXURE - 3B	P.No. 91
	ANNEXURE - 3C	P.No. 92
	ANNEXURE - 3D, 3E	P.No. 93
	ANNEXURE - 3F	P.No. 94
	ANNEXURE - 3G	P.No. 95
	ANNEXURE - 4,5,6,7,8,9	P.No. 96 to 105

FORE WORD

Suravaram Sudhakar Reddy,
Ex. - M.P.
General Secretary, CPI

New Delhi
Date : 20th September 2012

I am happy to know about the Biography of Sri Muchukota Venketaramaiah who is known as 'Grandhalayam Tataiah' in Kurnool during my childhood. Library movement played a very important role in our country in spreading knowledge and rousing consciousness, social, cultural, and political among the people. Literates were only a very small percentage in our population. Among the literate people, many could not afford to purchase books. Books were not costly comparatively but many people could not afford even that small amount in those days.

Some prominent people in our state also understood the importance of the library movement and they pioneered the movement.

I was born in Mahaboob Nagar District but my village was a border village of Kurnool District, hence we were staying in Kurnool for our studies. Before that I had my elementary education in a street school and a tuition master who knew only Telugu used to come and teach us at home, in our village.

From class III up to graduation, I studied in Kurnool. I had my law degree from Osmania University at Hyderabad and Joined Law Post graduation in Delhi University which I could not complete

In Telangana, no library could be established, no school in Telugu language could be established. In the composite Madras state in which Kurnool was a part, Libraries, schools were allowed to be managed by Private people. We were living in Narasimharaopet a lane behind Sri Venketaramaiah garu's house. I used to have a friend K.Sivabhushanam who was the son of the head master of Municipal High School, who used to live in the house opposite to Sri Venkataramaiah's house.

One day we saw the board "Andhra Grandhalaym" and peeped in, hesitatingly. We were invited inside and asked to sit in children's wing .Chandamama, Balamitra, Bala and many children's magazines were there. We got interested and then got addicted to it. We used to visit frequently and later started taking books also. That had a big impact on my life in later period. I got a nick name "Book worm", though I was good in hockey in ACC and other extracurricular activities.

Large number of children from neighbourhood and elders also used to visit that library which benefited them. We prefered going to library to going to films and to other activities like playing in parks etc. I am one among the lakhs of people who benefited and changed my lifestyle due to our habit of reading books in libraries. Library movement has spread in coastal Andhra and Rayalaseema with many private and public libraries coming up. Though Britishers allowed libraries, they did not give any monetary help to libraries or for constructing reading rooms. In state capitals they established big libraries, but filled them with British books.

After independence, Municipal libraries, District Central libraries have come up. Reading rooms were encouraged. But not much help was given to Private libraries.

It is in that Back ground that Sri Muchukota Venketaramaiah garu started a library in the front portion of his house. He was a teacher in Coles Memorial School where I studied 6th and 7th class.

I remember that "Andhra Grandhalaym" was the only Private library in the town. The other libraries used to have office time working hours which does not suit either employees or students. Andhra Grandhalayam used to function after 5 pm, which used to be very convenient.

As far as I remember, Sri Vanketaramiah garu did not have any assistant. He used to dust the Almairahs, books, maintain registers, used to issue books, and supervise the reading room. He used to wrap covers on all the books. He not only devoted all his life to library but sacrificed his property and his sisters' property to the cause of library. As he has to be present in the library after school hours, he sacrificed his family life and social life also. That was his devotion and love to the library movement.

This type of activity will not be acknowledged easily by the people. It looks like a "Thankless job". But he did not do if for appreciation or expecting some rewards. He did it as he believed it as his responsibility. He did it as his life mission. That is why he was regarded as a rare personality and commanded high respect from the people. I salute his memory with all affection and respect.

In the last few decades the library movement in India is in crisis. Though the Government collects money as library cess from people, it does not allot the funds properly. Thousands of librarian jobs are vacant, and tens of thousands of librarians are unemployed. Books have become costly. Good books are not purchased for libraries.

There are allegations of corruption on selection of books.On the other hand, reading habit among the people is going down alarmingly. Children and youth are addicted to TV channels.

Women who use to read, books, novels and magazines are now more interested in TV serials.

The government should try to revive library movement with all sincerity. More libraries should be established in rural and urban areas. Good books should be supplied. All the librarian posts should be filled up.

Sri Venkataramaiah garu is no more. But should be honoured. His photograph should be put up in District central library, at Kurnool. One library building should be named after him. His bust size statue should be installed in Narasimharaopet. This will be a small tribute to him. Reviving library movement will be the real reward to him.

I hope this small book on Sri Venkataramaiah garu and his contribution will be well received by all the book lovers and library lovers in our state. I congratulate his son Sri Chandrasekhar for his untiring efforts to bring to light his illustrious father Sri Venketaramaiah's contribution to library movement.

Suravaram Sudhakar Reddy,
Ex. - M.P.
General Secretary, .C.P.I.

KOTLA JAYA SURYA PRAKASH REDDY
MEMBER OF PARLIAMENT
(LOK SABHA) KURNOOL.

C1/3 THILLAK LANE, NEWDELHI-110001
Ph : 011-23782592, Mobile : 9490131222
RIVER VIEW COLONY, KURNOOL, A.P.
PH : 08518 - 248999, 224488

Member
Committee on Estimates
Committee on Water Resources
Consultative Committee on Petrolium&Natural Gas
Indian Council of Agriculture Research Society

FORE WORD

Sri.Venkataramaiah worked as a teacher and his name was prominently heard. He rendered his service in the form of Andhra Granthalayam and it was praised by one and all. The library inculcated the habit of reading in many children. In those days, libraries and public radio were main sources of information.

The library was established during 1923. Sri.Venkatarmaiah recorded the aim of starting Andhra Granthalayam as 'Serva Jana Sevaname Bhgavath Sevanam' meaning 'service to humanity is service to God'. He gifted his property to the library. He rendered this service from 1923 to1972.This book enables readers of other States to know the circumstances prevailed in Andhra Pradesh.

The book written by M.V.R.Chandrasekhar is a rich and glorious tribute to his father. The book will inspire present generation towards selfless social service and care for the needy and down trodden, particularly in these days of competition and degradation of moral values.

Kotla Jaya Surya Prkash Reddy

FORE WORD

Dr. Velaga Venkatappaiah,
Retired from Dept. of Public Libraries,
Government of Andhra Pradesh,
Tenali.

Dt. 23-8-2012.

It is really a privilege to write a foreword to a monograph on Shri Muchukota Venkataramaiah., who organized Andhra Granthalayam, Kurnool from1923-1972.He was one of the pioneers of Andhra Desa Library Movement and responsible for maintaining a public library without Government support. Infact, during freedom movement days, the people of Andhra Desa, though they were not rich enough, maintained public libraries, with the help of philanthropic people in the towns and even in small villages. A meager grant came through the government from 1922 onwards, with the strenuous efforts of Sri.Konda Venktappaiaha, Member of Legislative Council in the Composite Madras State. Even this offer Sri.Venkataramaiah did not utilise.This is his integrity and thinking level.

The unique feature of Sri.Venkataramaiah is that he allotted a part of his house for locating the library. He donated 20acres of land for the maintenance of the library. Besides, he worked as a librarian for about 50 years, without taking a rupee as remuneration. That is the greatness of Venkataramaiah. He is really a saint among common people. With simple living, high thinking and unstinted devotion, he became an idol of library community. Always dressed in Khadi Dhoti along with a sella, he reminded us of Mahatma Gandhi. With life ambition of spreading knowledge to common people, he justified his existence in this mundane world.

I had the great opportunity to see him, working in the library during 1970 and spend some time with him. That is the most memorable day in my life. I congratulate Mr.M.V.R.Chandrasekhar, son of Sri Venkataramaih, for bringing out this book with lot of details on the work and life of this great personality Sri.muchukota Venkataramaiah.

Dr. Velaga Venkatappaiah

Dt. : 5-10-2012.

Dr.K.Maddaiah, M.A., Ph.D, P.G.D.O.C.J,
Reader in History / Journalism
34/28-29,Peta,Kummari street,
Kurnool - 518001.
Cell : 9951121036, Ph : 08518 - 242106.
e-mail : kurabamaddaiah@gmail.com

FORE WORD

Sri.Muchukota Venkataramaiah (1894-1972) was a multifaceted personality-a nationalist, founder of Andhra Granthalayam, Scout and drawing master, a Telugu Pandit,a mellifluous singer and a true Gandhi an-all rolled into one.

He was associated with several nationalists like Gadicherla Harisarvothama Rao, Vanam Sankara Sarma, Kadara Badara Subbarao,O.Lakshmanaswamy, Dharani Ramachandra rao Nittore Ramaswamy and many other leaders from Kurnool district.

Though he hailed from Anantapur District, Muchukota village, Tadipatri taluk, he settled down in Kurnool district. His education in his native district, Coles Memorial High School, Kurnool and Pachayppa's college Madras moulded his career.

During the freedom struggle, he established Andhra Granthalayam at Kurnool on 1-8-1923.This library catered to the needs of the people of Kurnool town for fifty years. Promotion of Telugu literature, spreading of knowledge and the motto 'service to society is service to God' were the main objectives of his library. The library had a rich and rare collection of books on Telugu Literature, News papers, journals, Magazines and reference books. Many readers/ visitors to the library became celebrities after Independence and occupied high offices.

Sri.Venkataramaiah refused to accept the financial grant offered by the Government of Andhra Pradesh and ran it as a private library till his death. He donated ancestral property for the maintenance of library. Smt.Sindhiraju Venkamma, widowed sister of Sri. Venkataramaiah deserves a special mention as she too served the cause of library movement by gifting her inherited lands.

As an S.S.L.C. Student in 1969, I visited Andhra Granthalayam. Sri.Venkataramaiah was a strict disciplinarian and hence the board 'Silence Please' greeted me. He was a symbol of simplicity and dignity but commended lot of respect by the people of Kurnool town. He was wearing a typical Indian dress, spotless Khaddar Dhoti, a coat and a turban.

No account of the Library Movement in Andhra Pradesh would be complete without a reference to Andhra Granthalayam. His service to the cause of Library Movement in Kurnool District will be remembered forever by the future generations.

I am glad that the family members have decided to bring out a monograph in English, the translation of the original Telugu Book 'Grandhalayam Thathaiah'. I hope the monograph will be highly useful to the teachers, research Scholars', Librarians, Students and the general public.

I salute the great man of Rayalaseema who dedicated his life for Andhra Granthalayam, which created awakening among the people of Kurnool town.

Dr. K. Maddaiah,
M.A.,Ph.D, P.G.D.O.C.J

A TRIBUTE TO ANDHRA GRANTHALAYAM
BIOGRAPHY OF MUCHUKOTA VENKATARAMAIAH
CHAPTER - 1
INTRODUCTION

The words 'Andhra Granthalayam' mean Telugu Library. The word is also synonymous with Library Movement in Andhra Pradesh which was an integral part of Indian Independence movement. The typical Andhra Library was not a mere store-house of books but was a centre "from where all the healthy activities of the community, social, religious, literary and in some cases political also proceeded". A magazine with this name was published during the period 1939 to 1941, which inspired many volunteers and leaders. Some Libraries were established in Andhra desha with the name 'Andhra Granthalayam' of which Andhra Granthalayam, Kurnool was a jewel. It is special because it is mostly individual's effort.Composite Madras State before independence included present Tamilnadu, Kerala, Andhra and parts of Karnataka. The then Chief Minister of the State visited the Andhra Granthalayam.Many leaders associated with freedom struggle visited and blessed the library. This testfies significance and the importance of the Andhra Granthalayam in those days. The glory of this library is interwoven with the biography of Muchukota Venkataramaiah.

"Scores of living species breathe on the earth. Of all the species, the human being has a distinctive speciality-communication. Apart from communication, man is bestowed with expression, discrimination, wisdom, tact and creativity. With these God given gifts, man is dominating like a monarch, exercising control over the rest of the world. Humans look similar in appearance but their mental disposition is varied.

We come across different types of people. Some wish to live for themselves. Some wish to live with others. Great people live for the sake of others.

They perceive their life as a gift given by God and strive to achieve something that is useful to others. Such noble people leave their impression in history. They do not strive for fame. Muchukota Venkataramaiah belongs to such category of noble persons, who are selfless and who strive to help others" wrote Dr.Bharathi Gopalakrishnan, Saint Joseph High School, Kurnool about Venkataramaiah.

Venkataramaiah realized while he was very young that literacy rate in India was abysmally low and was responsible for all problems faced by his countrymen. He decided to contribute for the improvement of these conditions.He gave up his job in revenue department as a token of his dislike of foreign rule. He made "spread of education" his life's ambition . He did not aspire to obtain high degrees. He restarted his career as a teacher on obtaining minimum qualifications required, which gave him ample scope to fulfill his desire to impart education in those days of low literacy. Library movement provided him an opportunity to enhance his service arena.

Venkataramaiah started a public library, Andhra Granthalayam at Kurnool on 1-8-1923. He recorded the aim and objective of starting library in a registered gift document. The purpose is stated as 'Serva jana sevaname Bagavath sevanam'.The statement means that 'Service to Humanity is service to God'.

Venkataramaiah further stated that his intention was also development of Telugu literature. There was an absolute necessity of a public library at Kurnool . Only few people could afford to purchase newspapers and books during those days when Andhra Granthalayam was started. Central Library under local library authority started functioning only during 1953.

Venkataramaiah actively participated in library movement which is a part of National movement. He faced many challenges and suffered financial losses yet personally maintained Andhra Granthalayam. Local self government offered a little financial support to the libraries after 1922. After Independence, the government offered help to the libraries. Venkataramaiah did not seek monetary help from government. Reasons are not known. Probably he wanted to contribute to society to the extent passible to him. He maintained the library with his own resources till his last breath on 4-4-1972.

Venkataramaiah set apart a portion of his property for continuation of Andhra Granthalayam after him, as is done by parents for welfare of their children. His sister Smt.Sindhiraju Venkamma supported his endeavour and gifted her property in favour of Andhra Granthalayam.

Andhra Granthalayam disseminated information. During Second World War and other wars after independence, or any event of importance in the world, people thronged the library for information. Andhra Granthalayam attracted children in particular and is responsible for development of reading habit among them. The library also served the needs of ladies who did not have access to books. They were interested to know developments in the society and country. They had interest to guide their children. Telugu scholars optimally utilized the library. Andhra Granthalayam not only preserved general books but also stored all master pieces available at that time in Telugu and English. For youth aspiring to secure jobs by appearing for competitive examinations library offered all facilities.

Venkataramaiah did all the work related to Andhra Granthalayam for nearly fifty years from 1923 to 1972. As a devoted teacher and as a sincere librarian he enjoyed the services rendered by him.

He knew no other pleasure. There are so many leaders and volunteers that gave their might in every sense of the term to develop literacy and education. Venkataramaiah is unique among them.

Today is an era of dynastic successions where most of the achievers try to pass on their greatness and physical possessions to their children. Venkataramaiah being a true Gandhian did not seek recognition or power all his life. He never bothered about making money for himself for his children. He wanted his children to be servants of humanity. He always strived for the benefit of the society, increasing literacy. He believed in simple living high thinking and service to humanity which also formed the basis of Gandhian philosophy.

In this monograph I have made a humble attempt to place on record the recorded evidences of the precious services rendered by Venkataramaiah to enhance literacy and the Library Movement in Kurnool district. Venkataramaiah never craved for recognition.

To understand the biography of Venkataramaiah, one should recollect the circumstances that prevailed in the first decade of nineteenth century and the history responsible for such circumstances. An attempt is made to present a brief summary of such circumstances in chapter -2

CHAPTER - 2

HISTORY AND STATUS OF EDUCATION IN THE FIRST DECADE OF TWENTIETH CENTURY

India was an "invaders paradise" for many hundreds of years. Our country had to face the Greeks, the Huns, the Persians, the Turks, the Afghans, the Mongols, the Arabs and the British. The invaders in order to establish their rule tried to impose their culture and their way of life.Libraries and books formed personal property. Many libraries in the past vanished because of invasions, wars and negligence.

East India Company took advantage of weaknesses of the native rulers and established their rule. Unlike other invaders they did not prefer to become part of community. Their main interest was to take away wealth to their country. Religious sentiments in utilizing gun cartridges sparked off the first war of Independence. Freedom spirit was crushed by the East India Company. The British Crown realized the cruelty with which wealth was amassed. The Crown took over the administration in India from East India Company .Though siphoning of wealth was not given up administration was improved with certain degree of accountability.

Requirements of administration prompted rulers to introduce English education in the country. English education methods were introduced on three fronts. 1 .Christian missionaries started educational institutions with the idea of spreading their religion 2. British government started institutions as they felt that such institutions and English language will assist administration and strengthen British rule.3.Indian leaders thought that mass education will prepare India towards freedom.

Woods and Hunter commission submitted reports to British parliament in the years 1854 and 1882 respectively on needs of English education in India.

First World War made Europeans realize the importance of human values. They also realized that they were a minority and to rule a majority community they would have to address at least certain needs of Indians. Indians, who could afford, got educated and started examining the situation in the country. They understood that good governance meant freedom of speech, equality before law ,dignity of labour and self respect. These were denied to Indian citizens who were part of the British Empire. They thought that education would change the situation. Many believed in moderation.

They opined that all sorts of Governments have deficiencies. Adaptability of society to bad rule could be achieved with education. For the spread of education and knowledge, schools and availability of books were important. Till the end of 19th century, in many parts of the country there were single teacher, private street schools to impart literacy in many villages and towns. Availability of books was the main constraint and literacy was as low as 5%. To overcome shortage of books the leaders started Library Movement. One more important reason for starting Library Movement was the need to organize secret meetings and spread messages of freedom struggle.

CHAPTER - 3

ROLE OF VOLUNTEERS IN PEOPLE'S MOVEMENT

In any struggle undertaken for improvement of society role of the volunteers, their dedication, knowledge and the way in which volunteers reach masses are important to achieve goal of development. Leaders guide the movement.

Mahatma Gandhi defined a Volunteer as:-

"A Volunteer is someone who serves in a community or for the benefit of natural environment primarily because they choose to do so. Many serve through a non-profit organization - sometimes referred to as formal volunteering, but a significant number also serve less formally, either individually or as part of a group. Because these informal volunteers are much harder to identify, they may not be included in research and statistics on volunteering.

By definition, a volunteer worker does not get pay or receive compensation for services rendered. Volunteers don't necessarily have time, but they have the heart. As a volunteer, you will learn not just more about the needs of others, you will also learn more about your own needs and you will discover that in helping others, you help yourself most of all.

A Volunteer can be anybody. There are no age limits to being a volunteer, no preferred categories, any salary specifications, any special degrees or work experience. All that is required is dedication to the cause, sincerity about work that one is doing and commitment to a regular and sustained effort with the organization.

Muchukota Venkataramaiah was the personification of Mahatma's definition of the volunteer. He continued his effort in promoting knowledge through Andhra Granthalayam even after Independence.

Dr. Velaga Venkatappayya, Secretary (retired), District library Forum, Andhra Pradesh in his book written in Telugu "Granthalaya seva nirathulu", wrote:-

"Library service is sacred as it gives opportunity to serve without any personal benefit or self interest. Especially during independence struggle, knowing fully well that it is going to be a regardless and thankless job many people were inspired by their conscience and entered this sphere".

Among them Muchukota Venkatramaiah was one important and a dedicated librarian.

CHAPTER - 4

LIBRARY MOVEMENT

The British introduced "Sedition law", Section 124 A of Indian Penal code in 1860. They realized that libraries could be made use of in propagating ideas without attracting the attention of the government. So leaders of freedom struggle initiated library movement.

Venkataramaiah evinced interest in the Library movement from his school days. He was attending conferences whenever they were arranged. All Andhra library conferences were held every year. Leaders and volunteers from all over Andhra area attended the conference. Progress and impediments to the movement were discussed. Leaders communicated and discussed and proposed programs related to libraries, adult education, scout movement in particular and other programs meant for the development of society.

All India Library conference was held at Coconada (Kakinada) on 26-12-1924. Mr. M.R.Jayakar, Bar at Law, a representative from Maharashtra was elected as president. In his extempore presidential address he praised the library activities in Andhradesa and said *"The Andhra Public Library movement true to the genius of the race has maintained the best of the old institutions and incorporated so much of the new as is absolutely necessary. The typical Andhra Library is not a mere store-house of books but is a centre from which all the healthy activities of the village, social, religious, literacy and in some cases political also proceed*".

A lecture was given by Sir. Arcot Ramaswamy Mudiliar on 5-5-1928 on "Library Movement and Adult Education'. His ideas are relevant even today.

'Elementary education should be followed by reading good books to shape one to be a good citizen. Average graduate on entering the din and dust of life forgets the purpose of real education'serve the needy'. At every stage of life one should learn to improve their skills.' Sir.Ramswamy Mudiliar felt that Libraries and Adult Education serve these needs of society

In Rayalaseema, several 'Andhra Library Conferences were held. The 7th Conference was held at Mahanandi Temple town located in Kurnool District (1920), the 12th conference at Anantapur (1927), 24th Conference at Hindupur in Anantapur District (1943) and the 28th Conference at Chagalamarri of Kurnool District (1951).

Volunteers of library movement in Andhra were dedicated organizers. They formulated their own plans in furtherance of their programme and implemented them. Alien rule opposed the programme and viewed with suspicion. It is said that the government was collecting information through Intelligence Department about the activities of the libraries. Even the readers were under scanner.

For example, P.V.Narasimha Rao, our former Prime Minister, wrote a book with the title "THE INSIDER" in which he narrates his experiences in school. He was in the habit of reading books which inspire freedom spirit. The librarian of the school sent a secret report to the education officer who in turn advised the headmaster to warn the boy. The head master on enquiry was satisfied and so, no action was taken. In some cases students used to be discharged from schools when it was clear that they were pursuing literature related to freedom struggle

Library movement is unique as it laid foundation for literacy and adult education ("Sarva Siksha Vidhya Abhiyan"). Scout organization became part of library movement as it cultivated a spirit of service in children. It must also be said that many movements sprang up with Library Movement as leaders

Learned to reach masses. For example co-operative movement which liberated farmers from money lenders, farmer's movement which brought scientific methods in cultivation, swadeshi movement which generated income in villages, eradication of untouchables movement which is responsible for social enlistment of the downtrodden were initiated with the library movement.

Not supported by government in any form, volunteers of library movement mobilized the support of people and organized programs. Important of them were 1) Starting of new libraries in towns and villages and attracting people towards education 2) Striving for improvement of literacy 3)Providing more books to libraries 4) Securing funds for libraries.

Well informed people led the movement by inspiring the volunteers and guiding them. Leaders of the Library movement are known to the History and need to be respected.

Sri Kodati Narayanarao, a distinguished participant of Library Movement in an article published in the book "Andhra Pradesh Darsini" presented the role of library volunteers in library tours. Communicating information was difficult those days.Translated extract is presented here:-

"This forms important and unique form of publicity. Sri Ayyanki Venkataramanayya introduced this form. One firka (now known as mandal) or one taluk (Three to four mandals of present day revenue set up) is selected. Nearly twelve volunteers in six groups conduct this program in one week to a month.

First group visits the village and prepares the villagers to receive the volunteers.

Second group enters the village tours the village singing songs related to importance of learning. Third group organizes exhibitions. Fourth group attracts people with songs and other entertainments at the stage set. Fifth group makes arrangements for meeting.

Sixth group receives leaders, arranges lectures and all other necessities.

These efforts form a base for setting up of a library and selection of volunteers to conduct classes for children and adults. This type of efforts gave very good results in West Godavari ,Krishna and Guntur districts. During April and May when schools do not function students and teachers are free and during this Vasantha season. Celebrations related to libraries are undertaken to establish new libraries and strengthen existing libraries.'

Following table published in Granthalaya Sarvaswam depicts results of efforts of leaders and volunteers of library movement in opening new libraries.

Increase in Number of Libraries in corresponding year

Name of the district	1914	1915	1918	1919
Krishna	48	53	140	150
Guntur	34	52	130	160
Godavari	34	43	90	103
Nellore	10	16	28	30
Visakhapatnam	8	8	17	30
Ganjam	6	6	20	22
Cuddapah	3	4	4	7
Kurnool	2	2	3	3
Bellary	2	2	3	3
Ananthapura	2	5	10	15
Chittore	-	2	6	10
Nizam State	10	12	12	13
Madras	-	2	2	3
Rest of part of Andhra	4	5	9	13
Total	162	212	474	586

Mahatma Gandhi toured Rayalaseema during September and October 1921. The effective thrust of his speeches was on the eradication of untouchability and Swadeshi Movement. At Kurnool, a public meeting was organized on 30th September 1921. The second visit of Mahatma to Kurnool district was during May 1929. Both the visits had astounding effect on people's urge for freedom.

Volunteers of the Library Movement rejuvenated their energies and implemented program with greater commitment.

The Library movement achieved its objective. It subsisted with partial self rule and after independence it became subject of government. Before independence education department, adult education, total literacy program, scout movement and libraries formed one department. During 1935 adult education got separated, another wing 'Education for all', total literacy project got separated after Independence. Scout movement which inculcated service motive in children has become dormant. Ultimately libraries became a small part of education department.

STATUS OF THE LIBRARIES AT PRESENT :-

Education could become a successful business model. Libraries continued to be social welfare measures in planning of Government. Even after sixty five years of Independence, a qualified post graduate librarian can only become Deputy Director of libraries in Andhra Pradesh. Officers of primary education sector only can become the Director of libraries by opting for deputation as Deputy Director. They do not acquire any qualification required for maintenance of library or spend even a single day maintaining any category of library.

Libraries which are a century old viz. Saaraswathanikethanam, Sri Krishnadevaraya Andhra Basha Nilayam, Library at Sarvothama Bhavan are functioning efficiently under private management. Salaries are not paid on par with state librarians though teachers in aided schools get salaries on par with government teachers. Many great libraries must have become extinct for want of support. In recent times internet further diminished the importance of Libraries.

Still Libraries are the main source of knowledge for common man. General readers go to libraries for news papers and reading books. All political parties publish news papers. Every item of news is depicted in their own perspective. Readers evince interest in reading more than one news paper for their own analysis. Literature books are not attracting general readers.

In spite of so many efforts made by the government, illiteracy still prevails. Literacy rate stands at less than 40% in rural areas.

CHAPTER - 5

ANCESTORS OF VENKATARAMAIAH

Muchukota Venkataramaiah was born on 5-10-1894 in Muchukota village. Muchukota village forms part of Peddapappuru Mandal of Anantapur District of Andhra Pradesh. The village is about 15 kilometres from Tadipatri on Tadipatri Anantapur road. It is about 40 kilometres from Anantapur. Anantapur district is one of the acutely drought affected districts in India.

Muchukota was an Agraharam (village area given as a gift) donated by the Kings to the Brahmins. British took over the administration at the beginning of the 19th century. By 1894, only one Brahmin family was in the village.

Details about the ancestors of Venkataramaiah, were recorded in the Will preferred by Karanam Ramaiah, maternal grandfather of Venkataramaiah. The Registrar came to Muchukota village to register the will. Karanam Ramaiah knew law. He did not leave his property unauthorized. The will No.5 dated 22-06-1904 (Copy Annexure - 4) was witnessed by his both sons-in-law, Hanumantha Rao and Venkatarayudu.

Karanam Ramaiah had three daughters. The first daughter Smt.Maheswari was married to Velidindla Hanumantha Rao. He was the Circle Inspector of Police at Tadipatri in 1904. The second daughter was Smt. Eswaramma, a widow without children and the third daughter Smt.Meenakshi, mother of Venkataramaiah was married to Karanam Venkatarayudu. Following table depicts the family tree.

Karanam Ramaiah

Velidindla Subramanyam is son of velidindla Hanumantha Rao

Muchukota Venkataramaiah
Sindhiraju Venkamma
Son and Daughter of
Karanam Venkatarayudu

Venkataramaiah 's father Karanam Venkatarayudu and mother Smt. Meenakshi were pious people. They were respected by the villagers for their generosity and readiness to help the needy.

Maternal grandfather of Venkataramaiah, Karanam Ramaiah was held in high esteem by virtue of his own scholarly qualities and administrative abilities. He could read and write in Sanskrit, English and also was proficient in Telugu. He stood the test of time and was the owner of 500 acres of land at Muchukota village alone. His landed property spread across villages like Rayalacheruvu, Yadiki, Vemulapadu and Konuppalpadu of Tadipathri taluk, Peravali of Anantapur taluk and Burgula of Peapalli sub division in Kurnool district. Pious as he was, he constructed Ramalingeswara swamy temple on the hillock to the west of Varadayapalli, hamlet of Muchukota village. He gifted lands for the maintenance of the temple.

. Venkatarayudu was the son of Chandrasekhar, a relative friend of Karanam Ramaiah.Venkatarayudu was selected by Karanam Ramaiah as his son-in-law because he wanted Venkatarayudu to stay with him, assist him in his work.

Such practice exists even today in Andhra and is called "illarikam" which means the son-in-law lives in the house of his father-in-law as a member of father-in-law's household and also becomes the owner of father-in-law's property.

Chandrasekhar gave equal share of his property to Venkatarayudu along with other sons and gave adoption to a relative cum friend Bhattaru Venkatanarsu, who was rich and had no male child.Venkatarayudu relinquished his rights over the property given by his own father on attaining majority. The property he got on adoption was given to his sister, whose husband lost all property in a gamble. Giving away property given by real and adopted fathers was not appreciated by his father-in-law, Karanam Ramaiah. He by his will No.5 of 1904 gave his property equally to both of his grandsons Venkataramaiah and Subramanyam with the condition that they should serve the deity and maintain the temple he constructed. Karanam Ramaiah also thought that Venkatarayudu required guidance and support of Hanumantha Rao who enjoyed power, being a Circle Inspector of Police.

The entire property given to Subramanyam was sold away to meet the expenses to send his son who was also named Hanumantha Rao for his studies in England.

CHAPTER - 6

EDUCATION AND HOBBIES OF VENKATARAMAIAH

The elementary education of Venkataramaiah took place at Ammalladinne and at Tadipatri. Ammalladinne is located at a distance of about two kilometres from Muchukota. His secondary education was at Anantapur. He had his high school education at Kurnool.

Venkataramaiah was inspired by his teacher at Ammalladinne who was responsible for his interest in Telugu literature. Venkataramaiah at the age of sixteen wrote Sri Ramashathakam, a book consisting of 100 verses in Telugu depicting the story of Sri Rama. The small booklet was printed at "Sri Thyagaraya Sastrulavari Girvanabhasha Ratnakara Mudraksharashala", a printing press named after great classical music composer Sri Thyagaraja. The press was established with the aim of printing Sanskrit books. Sri Ramashathakam book was printed during 1910. The press was located at Madras (Chennai).

The booklet signifies Venkataramaiah's interest in Telugu literature. There were good facilities of printing only at Madras. The book was printed with the contributions collected from philanthropists of Varadayapalli village. It could be inferred that printing a book in those days was a costly affair and Varadayapalli villagers had a lot of affection for Venkataramaiah.

English transliteration of Sanskritised Telugu verse in the first page is as follows : (verses in Telugu script are given as Annexure - 3A.)

Sreerasthu

Sri Ramachandra varaprasadalabdha kavithva mahathva yasovirajithaarvelakulabdhi madhyasthitha Bhattar vamsakhya swetha dvipanthara kalpavrukshayamana venkatarayamathya garbha pushpa samjanitha phalopama sakala sajjna vidheya venkatarama namadheya kavivara praneethambaina

Sri Ramashathakamiyyadi

Sri Ramabhadra vidrumarunamruducharana samsevaa mahathva samlabdhaoodithandhrakavithva vidya dwithiya vagvaibhava samanvithakhila vidvathjana vidheya bheemarajaaswayaaombhonidhi Rajanarayana Rajathmajundunu Chandrahasabhudayadi grandha virchithanatha kusalundunu Amalldinne pradhamapatasalopadhyundunu nagu B. obularaja nama kavivaryuniche sarijudabadi varadayapura nivasula dhanasahayamuche madaras barur thyagarayasastrulavari girvanabhasharatnakara mudraksharasalayandu mudrimpabadinadi. 1910.

Summary of the first page is as follows :-

The book contains hundred verses on the life of Sri Rama. This is composed by the poet Venkatarama, son of Venkatarayudu of Auruvelaniyogi Brahmin sect. He is always obedient to the good and scholarly wise people.

The book was scrutinized by a primary school teacher of Ammalladinne, B.Obularaju. He is the son of Bhimaraju, brother of Ramaraju who composed Chandrahasabhudayam.

Verses and poems form important part of Telugu literature. Venkataramaiah was in the habit of composing verses and poems to suit immediate needs. He never bothered to get them printed. His interest was in primary and adult education and library activities might have subdued his literary interests and writing books.

Pidugu Sivaramaiah was a teacher at Municipal High School Adoni. He was popular for designing short hand script books in South Indian languages. His son P.S.R.Murthy, retired officer, State Bank of India informs that his father was a good friend of Venkataramaiah and a frequent visitor to Andhra Granthalayam. As a boy, he used to witness with curiosity, the conversations between his father and Venkataramaiah in Telugu verses and poems.

Venkataramaiah was a good artist.He drew pencil sketches. Most of his sketches used to be the figures of prominent leaders. Occasionally he used to draw scenes from epics.

In those days drama, Burrakatha, Tholubommalata (puppet show) and dance performances were the only popular public entertainments available. Venkataramaiah got influenced by the drama 'Droupadi Vastrapaharanam' a part of the epic Mahabharatham written by Thirupathi Venkatakavulu.The verses in this drama are very popular even to this day inspite of the fact that cinema overtook drama. He purchased all the eighteen parvas of the epic Mahabharatha with his savings of the money he got as a student.

On 20-03-1915, Andhradesa Granthalaya Conference was held at Rajahmundry. After the conference, a book containing the details of the then existing libraries was collected. Details of the libraries were published in a book with the title 'Andhra Desa Granthalayalu'. One library listed in the book existed with the name 'Sadhujana Samaja Granthabhandagaram" in Varadayapalli, hamlet village of Muchukota village. Probably this library created a spark in Venkataramaiah and he started evincing interest in the Library Movement. The book was available at Saaraswatha Nikethanam library,Vetapalem Prakasam District. Translated summary of the extract is presented here under:-

Anantapur district, Tadipatri Taluk

160 Village - Varadayapalli

Name of the library :- Sadhujana Samaja Grandha Bhandagaram

Secretary :- Ratnakaram Gangaraju

Year of establishment :- 24 - 12 - 1912.

Monthly expenditure Rs. 2/- *Balance Rs. 39/-*

Number of books :- 1) Telugu - 19 2) Sanskrit - 6.

Books read last year - 13 *Subscribers - 15*

Meetings arranged previous year - 4

Average daily visitors - 10.

Working hours - 10 A.M. to 4 P.M.

Information given will reflect the status of education, scarcity of books and literacy rate in a village with a population of 750. The title 'Sadhu Jana Samajam' indicates efforts made for social justice even before the return of Mahatma Gandhi to India from South Africa.

Venkataramaiah must have realised the importance of books in those days.

Gadicherla Harisarvothama Rao the first student to be rusticated and the first editor to go to jail in Andhra stayed at Tadipatri in those days. His influence may be responsible for the establishment of a library at Varadayapalli.

Venkataramaiah did his Intermediate and Diploma in Education and Arts at Pachayappa's College, Madras (Chennai). At times he used to describe the difficulties faced by him at Madras. Money was the main constraint. Because of World War I, the students were forced to use kerosene lanterns. He was in the habit of taking hot water bath. In the mess he was residing, such facility was not available.

He bought small kerosene lamp and a can. Keeping the lamp beneath the can filled with water he was reading his books and at the same time was getting hot water for his bath.

Mahatma Gandhi conducted many Nature cure experiments on himself, at South Africa, cheap way of improving health for common man-an act against cruelty against Animals. One such experiment is avoiding cow milk.

Venkatramaiah was not in the habit of taking milk products. Mess owner prepared all preparations with milk products which forced Venkataramaiah to consume milk products. Children in those days were not taking food outside their mess. The mess owner treated inmates with affection.

Venkataramaiah was a Telugu medium student till school final. In Intermediate the medium of instruction was English. Books were not readily available. He suffered as was the case with many students with village background.

CHAPTER - 7

KURNOOL, KARMA BHOOMI OF VENKATARAMAIAH

Kurnool town is the head quarters of Kurnool District. It is about 200 Kms from Hyderabad and now is well connected by road and rail.

Kurnool District along with other parts of Rayalaseema was ceded to the British during 1800 by Nizam to clear debts incurred by him. Debts have arisen on acount of charges lavied by East India company towards maintenance of Military troops stationed for protection of Nizam territory. The British only tried to recoup revenue from ceded districts. The Kurnool district was one of the farthest districts from the state headquarters and so did not receive proper attention regarding development.

Sir Thomas Munro, Governor General, died of epidemic during his stay in the district on 6-7-1827. His death drew attention of the government about the pathetic living conditions in the district. Illiteracy was one of the main reasons that caused epidemics.

Sri Venkataramaiah started living at Kurnool from 1918, when he was appointed as teacher of Coles Memorial School apart from his stay as a student.

During the presidential address of 7th library conference of Andhra area in 1921 at Mahanandi, it was brought to the notice of participants that the four Rayalaseema districts suffer because of very low literacy rates and the number of libraries were less than thirty and the status of Kurnool District was no better. The proceedings were conducted in Telugu and published in Granthalayasarvaswam.

Summary of presidential address is as follows:-

"The situation in Kurnool district is depressing. In Sirvella village during 'Nala' year, a library was started. The books available are only 94. Kurnool District is famous for its Vaishnavite Shrine, Ahobilam and Shivite Shrine, Srisailam. During the olden days Srisailam was a big city. During Buddhist dynasty a great social congregation existed at Srisailam. A university flourished during the reign of Andhra emperors. Great philosopher and analyst Nagarjuna stayed here for some time. Even during recent past kings of Aravedu dynasity patronized Telugu literature. Great poets like Pingali Suranaryudu resided here. Kumara Dhurjati, Surana, Andukula Venkaiah wrote masterpieces like Krishnaraya Vijayam and Narapathi Vijayam and dedicated them to local kings. So great is the history of Kurnool District. It is distressing to note that the library movement in the district is lagging behind. People of the district should rise, awake their brothers, establish new libraries and improve literacy in the district."

During 1919, there were only four Libraries in Kurnool district. The 28th Library conference was held in July 1951. The report published after the conference revealed that there were 49 Libraries in Kurnool District.

At Kurnool town five libraries existed :

1) Andhragranthalayam 2) Central Library Kurnool 3) Mufdut Thuleba Library 4) Central co-operative Library 5) Anantha Kondaiah Setty reading room.

CHAPTER - 8

REASONS FOR SHIFTING TO KURNOOL

There were some reasons talked about amongst family circles of Venkataramaiah and also in Muchukota village describing circumstances that prompted him to shift and settle at Kurnool.

1st possibility - Venkataramaiah mother was not happy with her father's decision to distribute property to her sister's son. Her husband was "Illarikapu Alludu" and was the only entitled person for the entire property. She asked her son, Venkataramaiah to seek a job and not to depend on the property given by her father. The importance her husband enjoyed got diminished.

After his Matriculationexamination, Venkata Ramaiah passed Karanam test and joined as clerk in taluk office, Tadipatri. He worked as a clerk for a period of six months. He did not like the work which supported and formed part of British government. Many people in those days gave up jobs as a token of patriotism.

Venkataramaiah continued his Intermediate education at Chennai. Prof. Rockwood was the Principal of Coles Memorial High School, Kurnool. The school was under the management of American Baptist church. Venkataramaiah had his high school education at Coles Memorial High School. Prof. Rockwood used to appreciate Venkataramaiah's sweetvoice,obedience, tolerance and preparedness to help the needy. He offered him a teacher's job. Venkataramaiah readily agreed and joined as a teacher. He was permitted to acquire educational qualifications later. He acquired Diploma in Education and in Arts at Pachaiappa's college Madras(Chennai).

He believed that Americans were not against India's freedom struggle. Teachers in those days were highly respected.

2nd possibility - Water was a scarce commodity in Muchukota. Kurnool is bestowed with ample supply of water. So he settled at Kurnool though Tadipatri on the banks of river Penna also had good water resources.

3rd possibility - His sister Smt.Venkamma was given in marriage to a resident of Kannamadakala in Ovrvakallu firka, Kurnool district. Nittore Ramaswamy ,a popular advocate,Chairman, Kurnool Municipality during the period 1920 to 1922 was his cousin's (Velidindla Subramanyam) father-in-law..To be nearer to his sister and relatives he settled at Kurnool.

4th possibility - Venkataramaiah and his brother-in-law were followers of Gadicherla Harisarvothama Rao, prominent freedom fighter. Venkataramaiah and his brother-in-law were interested to do something for the society. So Venkataramaiah settled at Kurnool. (His brother-in-law died at an early age.)

5th possibility - Venkataramaiah was in the habit of reading books in the forest guest house that was far away from village. One insane person in Muchukota village was in the habit of doing any mischief ,if he was given a paisa. Someone offered this insane person a paisa and asked him to tie Venkataramaiah with a rope and hit his head with a boulder. The insane person followed the instructions. Timely intervention of the watchman of the bungalow saved Venkataramaiah. The real culprit behind it could not be identified. This attempt of murder terrified Venkatarayudu.It is common to eliminate lone successor to weaken the rich family. His deep love for his only son made him to ask Venkataramaiah to stay away from Muchukota village and so he settled at Kurnool.

6th possibility - Agriculture in Muchukota village was a gamble because of vagaries of monsoon. Policies of British government never protected farmers. Even when lands were fallow, farmers had to pay land tax. During the war, government forcibly procured grains at extremely low rates. Venkataramaiah lost interest in agriculture. After the demise of Karanam Ramaiah management of lands posed a problem. Lands were leased out. As Venkatarayudu was soft by nature, his tenants were not paying rents properly. It was felt that there was no necessity for Venkataramaiah to stay at Muchukota as cultivation was given up by the family.

CHAPTER - 9

ANDHRA GRANTHALAYAM AT KOTHAPETA, KURNOOL FROM I923 TO 1935

It is mentioned by Sri Vavilala Gopalkrishnaiah, a freedom fighter, in a report that an Andhra Granthalayam was started by Dharani Ramachandra Rao in 1920. (further information is not available about this library.)

Vavilala Gopala Krishnaiah, as head of a committee constituted by Government of Andhra Pradesh, visited Andhra Granthalayam at Narasimharaopet on 23-10-1979 and recommended for financial assistance from the government .However in his report 'Andhra Pradesh lo Grandhalayodyamum' he failed to mention about the Andhra Grandhalayam founded by Venkataramiah.

Venkataramaiah started Andhra Granthalayam on 1-8-1923. As an individual he used to call himself as teacher Muchukota venkataramaiah, S/o Karanam Venkatarayudu, but as library volunteer he used to function as M.Venkataramaiah, Manager, Andhra Granthalayam.

Venkataramaiah started his library in a hall with dimensions of 13/19 feet. The hall was on the first floor of the then house No. 41-193 of Kurnool Municipality.

The following information about 2nd anniversary of AndhraGranthalayam is collected from magazine, Dharma Granthalaya Patrika preserved at Harisarvothama Bhavan library at Vijayawada.

Translated Extract from Dharma Granthalaya Patrika, September 1925 :- Venkataramaiah celebrated the 2nd anniversary of Andhra Granthalayam on 15-8-1925 with all pomp at Coles Memorial High School ,Kurnool. The function started at about 5.30 P.M.

O. Lakshmana Swamy Bar-at-Law and Chairman Kurnool Municipality presided over the function. The function was started with a prayer followed by praise of poets in the form of verses as was customary in those days. The Boys of the High School enacted a play "Shakuna Achara Prahasanam" witten by the famous social reformer Kandukuri VeeresaLingam Panthulu. (The play condemned the wrong notions and bad customs in society.) K. Annamaraju, a teacher from Gadidamalla (Gargeyapuram) explained the usefulness of libraries. K.Narayana Rao gave a lecture on poets of Datha Mandlam (Rayalaseema). Ch. Narasimham spoke about the poet Thimmana and Municipal High School teacher V.Subbaiah gave a lecture about the greatness of poet Pothanamathyudu. Doma Venkata Swamy Gupta, Telugu Pandit from Koilakuntla gave a lecture on poet Srinatha. The verses were sung with a sweet voice. The audience enjoyed the verses and his sweet voice.

Venkataramaiah read the Annual Report of the Library. During 1925-1926, 5018 readers attended the library. 4016 books were issued. An amount of Rs150 As. 14 Ps.0 was collected in the form of subscription. Venkataramaiah's contribution and donations accounted for Rs.160 As.8 Ps.0. The total expenditure since inception on 1-8-1923 on library was Rs. 808 As.14 Ps.4.

The assembly was informed that Panagal Raja P. Rama Rayaningar, Chief Minister of Madras State, well known devotee of Sri.Rama Vavila kolanu Subba Rao,,and M.V.Venkateswarlu visited and blessed Andhra Granthalayam.

Earlier Andhra Granthalaya Bala Saraswathi Parishad conducted competitions for the students. The prizes were distributed to the winners.

The topics for the competition for the next year were also announced - Verses from Rukmini Kalyanam from verse 80 onwards and Bharathiyuni Kathalu (Indian Moral Stories). Venkataramaiah further announced that a written examination and elocution competitions would be held for upper three classes of High School of Kurnool Students during the first week of July1926. Entrance fee was fixed at four Annas. First prize was declared to be a medal made of gold weighing half a tula (6 grams).Topic for the test was from a book written by Sonti Ganga DharaSasthry," The great Warrior of Maha Bharatha 'Arjuna'".Function continued till 8-30 P.M. in the night. Gadicherla Harisarvothama Rao, District Inspector of Schools Peraiah Sasthry, Prof.Rockwood Princepal, Coles Memorial High School, lawyers, employees, land lords, and students attended the function. The function concluded praising donors and participants with a vote of thanks

Gadicherla Harisarvothama Rao was a great freedom fighter. Some information about Very important persons mentioned is detailed in Annexure 1.

After having maintained Andhra Granthalayam for three years, Venkataramaiah thought that the good institute he founded, praised by everybody and useful to so many should function even after him. He wanted to provide permanent accommodation and funds for its maintenance.

In the gift deed No.1024. Dt. 12-7-1926, (Annexure - 5) Venkataramaiah recorded that he started Andhra Granthalayam on 1-8-1923. The aim of starting Andhra Granthalayam was recorded as "I have firm belief that Sarva jana sevaname Bhagavath Sevanam".

The intention of starting the library was also to develop Telugu language and spread of knowledge in the society".

Along with the hall which was on the first floor of the then house No. 41-193 of Kurnool Municipality owned by him, he gifted the following lands in Chinnkopperla village of Koilakuntla taluk of Kurnool district to the library. It is further mentioned that in case difficulty arises regarding property given, another property of equal value is to be set apart for the library.

SNo.	Kushki/Enam	Survey No.	Acers.Cents	Rs.An.Ps.	Name	Dir.
1	D	Part 221	2.43	1-3-6	Chouti chenu 1/2	North
2	D	Part 229	2.58	5-2-6	Nallvagu chenu 1/2	North
3	D	Part 241	6.47-1/4	12-15-3	Chandraiah chenu 1/4	North
4	D	Part 237	0.97-1/2	1-15-0	Thirugugadda 1/2	East
5	D	Part 235	0-13	0-4-0	Thirugugadda 1/2	East

The gift deed was witnessed by Prof. B.J. Rockwood, the then principal of Coles Memorial High School, Kurnool and Sri O. Lakshmana Swamy, Bar-at-Law.

Smt. Sindhiraju Venkamma, sister of Venkataramaiah also gifted lands in Pulluru village of Alampur Taluk Mahaboobnagar District with an extent of 12 acres bearing survey numbers 362A and 379/2 to this library.

The book "Endaro Mahanu bhavulu" meaning many great people written by Dr. M. Subbarao, contains the names of Venkataramaiah and Rockwood and they were described as detailed hereunder :

"Coles High school was established by the American Baptist Church. Mr. Rockwood was the then principal of the school and he used to appreciate the noble qualities of Venkataramaiah for his punctuality and earnestness in training the students in fine arts and other related subjects.

He established "Andhragranthalayam" in his own house and nurtured it by his own contributions by financing the purchase of periodicals. Rockwood, the principal was very much pleased with his charitable nature and donated some of his own books to Muchukota Venkataramaiah for having free access to the readers and school children in the local Andhragranthalayam located in Kurnool. Further he purchased all available published Telugu books and handed over to his library. He was partly responsible for modernizing the library. Established in his own house, this library had preserved many ancient texts on various subjects. An alphabetical index with code number for each book was given in a neatly arranged manner for the convenience of one and all. He was a very dignified and disciplined in all his actions in running the library with great attention to detail".

With Registered document No : 255 of 1926 Dt. 21-2-1926, Sri Venkataramaiah, purchased a house with an area of 3.5 cents with the then municipal number 41-278. Intention of purchasing house was not mentioned. He was in posssession of this house before he executed the gift deed on 12-7-1926. Probably he purchased this house for some other purpose. This was an independent house on the main road so was accessible to all. He gifted this house in lieu of hall with dimensions 13 feet /19 feet with the registered document No.1262 of 1926 Dt. 24-8-1926 (Annexure - 6). No mention is made as to why the change in gift was made within a month (between 12-7-1926 and 24-8-1926).

He incurred expenditure on registration which was expensive so it can be inferred that he had done it under pressure. One possibility could be the objection raised by neighbours about the various visitors to the Library. When a library is for the public, readers of all castes are bound to visit it. In those days Harizans (now daliths) were treated as untouchables.

Many Harizans were attracted towards Christianity because of ill treatment (untouchability) prevailing against them. Mahatma Gandhi vehemently opposed ill treatment of Harizans. Till about 1935 the library continued in the house bearing the then Municipality number 41-278.

Vanam Shankara Sarma a resident of Pattikonda Village of Kurnool District was a freedom fighter. He wrote about the Independence movement in his fortnightly news paper 'AINDRAVATHI'. The editorial article he wrote on the speech made by Sardar Bhagath Singh attracted displeasure of the British Government. He was prosecuted and fined for publishing the article. Sri Vanam Sankara Sarma did not pay the fine as it amounted to acceptance of crime. He closed the press and restarted it with the name Saraswathi press and published another news paper with the name 'HITHAWADI'. He continued publishing the paper even after Independence.

Sri Sieripi Anjaneyulu was a resident of Dharmavarm village of Anantapur District. He was a famous volunteer of Library movement. In those days volunteers conducted tours with the idea of collecting information about the progress of the movement and to report the same to the leaders. During his tour Seiripi Anjaneyulu visited Andhragranthalayam. His report in Telugu was published in Aindravathi and was reprinted in periodcal Granthalaya Sarvaswam. Aindravathi paper is not available.

Granthalaya Sarvaswam in digitized form is available at Sarvothama Bhavan Library in Vijayawada and University of Hyderabad. Summary of the report is as follows:-

1929 : As I went to Kurnool Town, I came to know of one fine and well functioning Library 'ANDHRA GRANDHALAYAM'.

I reached the Library at 7:00 P.M. and found the library activities going on. Inspite of being a small and compact one, it appeared to be an exemplary library in the entire Rayalaseema region. It was indeed a pleasant feeling to be inside the library. The library in charge M.Venkata Ramaiah was an enthusiastic, devoted young man who seemed to be selfless, kind and humble.

I came to know that he not only established this library but also funded and maintained it. The building in which the library is housed is owned by the library. 10 acres of land was set apart for its maintenance. With in six years of its establishment this 'abode of knowledge' had accumulated more than 3000 books in Telugu and English. The various books were carefully arranged in glass door almirahs. The librarian's involvement was reflected by the display of a treasure trove of books. Suggestions for improvement include procurement of "Talapatra Grandhalu", arranging propaganda techniques through Burrakatha, Harikatha, Tholubommalaatalu (puppet show) etc. to attract readers and encouraging reading habit apart from improving literacy.

CHAPTER - 10

ANDHRA GRANTHALAYAM AT NARASIMHARAOPET

Even today Narasimharaopet is considered to be a posh colony. The colony took shape around 1930. Venkataramaiah purchased two plots. Length of the plots was 90' and width was 60'. Both the plots faced north with roads abutting north and western directions. They were with aerial extent of 540 square yards.

Venkataramaiah first constructed a house for his residence which bears today the Municipality numbers 43-92 and 93. He shifted his residence to that house during 1935. Andhra Granthalayam was temporarily shifted to this house and started functioning. He started constructing the building for Andhra Granthalayam in the other plot which took shape by 1941 with ground and first floors.

The house 41-278 gifted to library in Kothapeta was vacant for a considerable period and so he sold the house on 11-11-1940.

The purchaser stated that he was cheated as the house sold was gifted to Andhra Granthalayam. To overcome the allegations and as required by the purchaser Venkataramaiah in gift deed No .123 of 1941 Dt. 22-01-1941 (Copy Annexure - 7) further gifted the following lands in favour of Andhragranthalayam. Earlier gift deed provides such facility.

These lands also are located at Chinnakopperla Village of Koilakuntla Taluk of Kurnool District.

S.No	Kushki/enam	Survey.No.	Acres-cents	Rs-As_Ps.
1	D	1/2Part124	5.84	11-11-0
2	D	1/2Part153	0.28	0-5-6
3	D	Part180	5.22	10-7-0
4	D	Part181	0.33	0.10-6
5	D	Part18	1.2	2-4-0
6	D	233/1	2.3	2-9-0

The purchaser reopened the issue and filed a suit O.S.No : 113/1941 in the court of law on 9-4-1941 (Copy Annexure - 8). Legal implications of the case :- Gift given to God cannot be restored. In this case Donor and Donnie are same. Provisions to change property are made in deeds 1024 and 1262. To satisfy the purchaser and as required by him, Venkataramaiah executed cancellation of gift deed in his own hand writing in the document with register number, 1262 Dt. 24-8-1941.

1) I have shifted my residence from Kothapeta to Narasimharaopet as a result of which, the maintenance of library has become inconvenient both for me or for my family members 2) The library does not have funds to employ separate sweeper for cleaning the library or a watchman for safety when the library is not functioning (as both these get attended to as a family job when library is located in the premises where Venkataramaiah is living). 3) No provision of funds is available for payment of house tax and water tax 4(a) When the library is not functioning children are entering the premises by climbing walls and are creating mischief 4(b) Compared to Kothapeta, Narasimharaopet is spacious, hygienic and is more lauded 4(c) Employee houses, hostels, educational institutions are located in Narasimharaopet as such it is more suitable for library

4(d) Sometimes children open taps and drenching surrounding area and creating nuisance 5) For expanding library the space is not sufficient 6) The house is uninhabited, so the neighbours are throwing garbage and other material before the house 7) The house does not have bathroom and latrine facilities as such it is not fit to be let out to families 8) There are no funds to appoint separate librarian 9) Library functions from 5 P.M. to 7 P.M. and during winter days returning home is difficult as such I am cancelling the gifting of the house.

The narration made in the document is indicative of the compulsions that troubled his mind.

During those days Venkataramaiah lost his wife Smt. Parvathamma and his younger daughter Janaki of 10 years age. The cause of wife's death is not known but daughter Janaki died of jaundice.

Venkataramaiah was in the habit of going on tours related to library movement. His father Venkatarayudu was not happy with the litigations he had to face and tours he was making. He felt that Venkataramaiah was neglecting his family. He was not against service but was against unnecessary litigation.

He did not like sale of lands for payments related to litigation. All the property in fact was owned by Venkataramaiah. Venkataramaiah could not act against the wishes of his father. Venkatarayudu wanted his son to take care of the only daughter Saraswathi. He insisted that he should marry again. Initially Venkataramaiah was opposed to the idea of marriage at that age but gave in as his mother, father and sister insisted. In those days marriage at that age was not uncommon. Probably Venkataramaiah did not feel such loneliness in life. His father mother and sister who supported his endeavour and gifted her lands for his library were not with him. He married Lakshmidevamma.

The purchaser wanted the house to be taken back giving him the cost and other expenditure incurred by him alleging that Venkataramaiah cheated him. Venkataramaiah refused to be called a cheat and was not prepared to take back the house. Those were the days of famine and world war. Even before the case came up for hearing Venkataramaiah was dragged to street panchayath. Street panchayaths were organised to 1) Harass weak taking advantage of depressing situation. 2) Devalue property and grab it. 3) Overcome legal implications. Dragging to steet panchayat was planned taking advantage of the debt made by Venkataramaiah from Anantha Naganna Setty in the construction of new house Andhragranthalayam.

Anantha Naganna Setty presided over the panchayath conducted on 22-11-1941. As per the decision of panchayath Venkataramaiah had no option but to pay back the value of the house along with fine and interest. In this deal Venkataramaiah lost the house constructed for Andhra Granthalayam. The house was with the then mucipality number 43/91 which had an area of 540 sq. yards and had ground and first floors. The house was sold to the street panchayat head family member, Anantha Kondaiah s/o Anantha Gantaiah.

Venkataramaiah signed the sale deed No. 828 Dated 11-5-1942 (Copy Annexure - 9). Thus Venkataramaiah suffered the worst period in his life from 11-11-1940 to 11-5-1942. Even his father who loved him did not come to his rescue. The only mistake committed by him was that he did not register property of equal value and cancel gift deed before selling the house. Second World war period was also a period of great suffering even for Venkataramaiah.

Later after about fifteen years the house was purchased by K.E.Madanna M.L.A. father of K.E. Krishnamurthy, present M.L.A. Dhone and Ex. minister of Andhrapradesh.

Thus the greatest dream of Sri Venkataramaiah to establish big and separate building for Andhra Granthalayam could not become a reality. The litigation must have eroded to some extent the confidence in the pursuit of noble cause of Venkataramaiah. Society remained as a silent spectator and did not come to his rescue.

In spite of all depressing happenings which humiliated him, Venkataramaiah was not disheartened. Andhragranthalayam continued in the house bearing numbers 43-92 and 93 Narasimharaopet till 1979. The house in which Venkataramaiah was residing was restructured to suit the needs of library and his residence. The front portion housed Andhra Granthalayam and the rear portion his residence.

When he was attending school routine of Venkataramaiah was same normally. He got up at 4A.M.After bathe he used to recite Ranganatha Ramayana in loud voice for about half an hour. Later he attended library work till 8 A.M. After prayer he was available to talk with visitors either relatives, or people that come from villages for treatment.

He was in the habit of preparing and setting teaching material for that day. By about 10.15A.M.horse cart used to stand before his house to take him to school. If the cart was late he would walk to school. He was a swift walker. In the evening after coffee he attended library till 7.P.M.

Dr.C.P.Viswanatham M.B.B.S.,M.S.Professor of ANATOMY(retired) expressed his reminiscences during 2012 as, "Those were my school and inter study days, pre and post Independence days (1944-1952) of exciting hectic activity. Venkataramaiah was back donor neighbour of mine.

Books were issued to be read at home.especially by women in the neighbourhood, who could not Persue higher studies. College women were rare among women unlike the present day when girls outnumber boys in Medial, Dental, Nursing colleges. In the night at 8 to 9 P.M., after dinner, he and his many contemporary neighbours used to gather at the library to discuss and exchange ideas on various news items of those hectic days. My uncle a medical practitioner was one among them. During this time he used to tend the books which were partly torn or damaged. I watched on number of occasions the way he was attending to them. It Was like a mother tending her infant child.

During holidays Venkataramaiah visited neighbouring villages to promote libraries and encourage education programs. The house plot had an area of 540 Sq.yards and the plinth area of the building was 3100 Sq.feet. Andhragranthalayam occupied about 1500 Sq.feet. It had two sections.

First section Free reading Room -Tables and benches to accommodate 15 members were arranged in this section. A minimum of three English, three Telugu dailies and the state and central publications which are freely supplied to libraries are placed in this section. This section functioned from 7 A.M to 9 A.M and 5 P.M to 7 P.M. till Venkataramaiah was in service.

Second section Books division -This section functioned from 5 P.M to 7 P.M. The readers did not have direct access to the books.(closed access system) Catalogues were available with broad classification of category and alphabetically arranged book list.

As indented by the readers, Venkataramaiah was identifying and delivering the books. For those who desired to read in the library premises no fees was charged. For those who wished to take the books to their homes Rs. 2was the deposit and Rs1 was monthly subscription.

Sahitya Academy award is is given to famous writer Tripuraneni Gopichand. He resided at Narasimharaopeta, when Kurnool was Capital of Andhra State 1953-56. His daughter Rajini (now Katragadda Rajani Subrahmanyam) was about ten years those days. She narrated her experience at Andhragrandhalayam. She wanted children Telugu magazine 'Papayee'. She wrote 'yee' vowel as consonant. Venkataramaiah took interest and patiently corrected her noting and saw that she rewrites the word. She also recollected the parental affection he had in advising children to reach home before it is dark. Those days streetlights performance was not good.

Mostly School children preferred to read in the library. For them two to three copies of magazines like Chandamama, Balamitra, Bala were made available.Efforts to cultivate the habit of reading among children used to be the main focus.Those who wished to take books home were of two categories. First category readers preferred easy reading books viz. weekly magazines like Andhra Patrika, Andhra Jyothi, Andhra Prabha and novels.

Second category of readers were serious scholars, students of literature or others fields of importance. Lovers of Telugu literature preferred verse, prose, drama books apart from magazines like Bharathi. Readers seeking employment and those pursuing competitive examinations sought separate books.

Important types of Telugu literature books that were available can be inferred from following details.

Dr.G. Damodram Naidu, Professor (retired) Telugu S.V. University informed that Andhra Granthalayam stored classics like Manudhramasastram, Vidhyrthikalpatharuvu, Poorva Gadhalahari, Kalyana Kalpavalli, Valmeeki Ramayanam with wordwise meanings and summary, Puranas, apart from variety of dictionaries.

Noted Telugu literate historian Vaidyam Venkateswaracharyulu referred to availability of books like Golkonda Patrika, Publications of Telugu classics with commentaries by Gadwal and Wanaparthy Samsthanas like Dharmasindhuvu, Yekshaganalu, Reddy Kula Nayakula Charitra.

Sahithya Rathna Heeralal informs that rare books like Veda Bhoogolam were preserved. Many Research scholars pursuing Telugu literature made good use of Andhra Granthalayam.

P. Balasubramanyam, joint Director retired, Government of A.P. neighbour observed and drafted during 2012 about Andhragranthalayam, Venkataramaiah started library with Mythological, Puranic books along with popular novels like Bhoothgruham, Aggiramudu, etc,. Number of news papers like like The Hindu, The Mail, The Indian Express, Andhrapatrika, Andhraprabha, magazines like Chandamama, Bharathi were subscribed. Film India which later became Mother India edited by Baburaopatel was a novelty eagerly waited by public. Only three to four members used to subscribe for the magazine. Venkataramaiah shunned publicity and was not given a sufficient identity in current decades.

Till the time district Central Library came into existence in 1953 Andhragranthalayam served the needs of the readers of Kurnool and surrounding areas. Reference Books were permitted to be read at the library only. Publishers were often collecting rare books that were not available for reprinting and were returning the same.

If an educated man is asked “How many libraries have influenced your career?

He may cite school, college, and university and or city library. Nobody remembers the librarian, particularly in open access system. Some books were read at library. Generally a reader selects all books related to subject he is interested. To avoid going to racks repeatedly one takes all the books and sits before a table. None tries to put them in the respective places after using the books. It becomes the duty of the librarian to keep the books removed and laid on tables in proper places so that the next day when another reader comes he can easily locate the book. A responsible librarian attends to the repairs of books with the help of an assistant if provided or by himself if one is not provided in his section.

Even in closed accession system the work load in libraries gets multiplied as it becomes the duty of the librarian to issue books and later keep them in proper racks after they are returned. To attend to the issue of books, collection of returned books and keeping them at respective places multiply work load. With usage, books require frequent mending Century old libraries like Saraswathanikethanam, Krishnadevaraya Andhrabhasha Nilyam maintained by Philanthropists follow closed access.

Venkataramaiah attended all work of library mostly without assistance. He on arrival of any new book was stitching the same with twine thread so that it remains intact for a long time, wrap it with thick brown wrapper. He examined every book returned and was carefully attending to the damages immediately. The books were classified into twenty sections such as poetry, prose, drama, history, science, law etc.

Maintenance of a library involves a lot of expenditure sometimes not possible for a family. Almost till 1975 getting news papers was considered to be wasteful expenditure.

Many were getting satisfied by hearing radio news broadcast from public places like parks, panchayat, municipal offices etc. Facilities were provided to read news papers at free reading rooms, offices, boards in public places. Even in Narasimharaopet which was considered to be a posh locality then, very few people were subscribing to news papers and magazines.

Venkataramaiah continued conducting annual function every year. He was in the habit of conducting competitions in reciting verses, elocution, and written test on current topics among the children and distributing prizes to the winners. He was preparing annual report and presenting the same in a meeting. Such reports were sent to magazine Granthalaya Sarvaswam and were published during 1952 - 55.

Summary of a few Annual Reports of Andhra Granthalayam Published in Granthalaya Sarvasvam are as follows :-

Years 52 - 53.

Periodicals Subscribed - Monthly magazines : 14 Weekly magazines : 3 Daily News papers : 5
The Free reading Room with news papers functioned from 7.A.M to 7 P.M.Number of visitors for the free reading room on the average were 72.
Number of books received by the readers on the average per day were 64, of which 39 were read at library and 25 were taken to home.
Amount received as subscription : Rs.181 As 11 Ps 6,

Contribution of the Secretary : Rs.387 As11 Ps.0.

Expenditure incurred : News papers :Rs.176 As2 Ps0.
Monthly and weekly Magazines : Rs.186 AS4 Ps0.
Purchase of Books : Rs.123 As15 Ps6.
Electricity: Rs.46 As14 Ps0.
Wages for the Assistant : Rs.36 As8 Ps0.

Years 53 - 54

Total books available : 5625.
The Free reading Room with news papers functioned from 7.A.M to 7 P.M.
Average monthly readers that attended library : 82.
Books were read at library, and were issued to home on alternate days and on the average total books issued per day were 34.
Yearly Expenditure : Rs.574 As6 Ps 9.
Contribution of Secretary Venkataramaiah was Rs. 378 As 7 Ps 3.

Year 54 - 55.

The library is being maintained by Vangmayodharaka Venkataramaiah since 32 years.

Total Books available : 5658.

The Free reading Room with news papers functioned from 7.A.M to 7 P.M.

Periodicals Subscribed - Quarterly Magazines : 8 Monthly magazines : 12 Weekly

magazines : 3 Daily News papers : 5.

Library books division was kept open from 5.30 P.M.to 7.00 P.M. On even days books were issued to home and on odd days books were issued to be read at library. Thus on 177 days 21 (2 English books) books were issued to be taken home and on 181 days days on the average 45 books (5 English) were issued to be read at library.

Amount collected in the form of subscription : Rs.289 As4 Ps0.

Contribution by Venkataramaiah Rs.406 As7 Ps0.

Expenditure incurred : towards magazines and news Papers : Rs. 343 As1 Ps0.

Wages : Rs.177 As5 Ps0.

Electricity : Rs.46 AS14 Ps0.

Total Rs.645 AS11 Ps0.

From 1952 to1955 average monthly expenditure of Andhra Granthalayam Rs. 390/- was equal to the salary of a lower division Government servant.The cost of 10 grams of gold varied from Rs.73 to Rs.91. Services rendered by Venkataramaiah cannot be valued.

After world War -1 efforts were made to provide funds to the libraries. Though the funds were meagre,the funds could sustain few libraries that could approach the government and follow procedures per se involved.

Venkataramaiah did not seek funds. One reason could be grants restricted freedom. There were many complaints of harassment. Granthalaya Sarvaswam recorded some. Local Library Authority tried to suggest some procedural changes, which were printed in the magazine.

At Vetapalem a small Village in chirala Mandal of Prakasam district a public library was founded during Library movement and named as Saaraswatha Nikethanam.

This library functions even today and fulfils the needs of various sections of the people.Probably it is maintained in a better condition compared to many government libraries in respect of old records and records are being digitised.Research scholars working on the history and culture of Andhra Pradesh regularly visit this library.

Existence of such libraries is the result of grants sought, support extended by local people, determination of self less organizers, and not the least functionaries of library.

Leaders of the library movement changed strategies with changing times. After Independence leaders felt that public libraries could not be sustained by individuals or group of people. Their efforts were mainly directed to organize State funded libraries and they recommended merger of private libraries with government libraries. In most cases the instructions of leaders were followed. Venkataramaiah deviated from these instructions. He had independent views. Restrictions that follow grants and failure reports of some functionaries could have influenced him. Elders capable of influencing him did not persuade him , giving respect to his views and age. American Coles Management a source of inspiration to Venkataramaiah left the country.

During early 1950's children library was planned in Narasimharaopet. Director of libraries advised through local authorities to take over the Andhragranthalayam. On their part it was informed that efforts would be made to name the library after Venkataramaiah, rent would be paid for accommodation. If possible one of the family members would be given job. The need for searching separate premises could be avoided. Venkataramaiah did not concede.

CHAPTER - 11

VENKATARAMAIAH AS TEACHER IN COLES MEMORIAL HIGH SCHOOL, KURNOOL.

Venkataramaiah was a teacher in Coles Memorial High School, Kurnool. Teachers in those days were highly respected. Most of the teachers deserved that respect as their only vocation then was to recognize talent in students and guide them to be worthy of this country.

One incident that occurred during 1953-54 in Coles Memorial High School could be cited as an example. Kurnool became the capital of Andhra State and new sections were opened in school to accommodate in flow of students. I was in 6th class, then called 1st form. The Hindi teacher was strict. He used to give home work and used to examine home work books of all students. He was striking with folded fist, so that the ring touched the head which was giving great pain. One newly admitted boy with timid looks was allotted first bench as he was short.

During the next class, on getting seated, Hindi teacher asked for home work books. New entrant had no reply and so received a blow. He started weeping. Other students informed that he was a new entrant. Teacher shouted 'Why did you not tell?' Another blow was given. During interval students surrounded the new entrant. They felt very happy to know that he was Chief Minister's son Krishna Reddy. They explained to him the cruel treatment they got from the teacher and requested him to inform his father and see that the teacher was dismissed. Krishna Reddy did not attend the school for the next two days. When he returned on the third day students enquired whether their request was conveyed to his father or not.

Without giving any reply he gave invitation for a party to be held on the next day and asked students to come prepared to go to a movie.

On hearing about movie every one forgot all issues. Next day during the party, the Chief Minister Bezawada Gopala Reddy personally came to the students and informed that Krishna Reddy was caned for calling his Hindi teacher with wrong words and so he could not attend school for two days. He further advised that teachers should be respected and should never be addressed without respect. Children learned their lesson and continued to enjoy the party. Such was the regard and respect given to the teachers in those days.

At school Venkataramaiah never engaged himself in long conversations. For enquiries he used to respond with short replies. If he was not in class he was sure to be found in the library.

Venkataramaiah retired on 29-7-1955. Some of his students could be contacted. Significant reminiscences are detailed here under :-

Mynampati Bhasker, is now a resident of Hyderabad. He is a popular news paper columnist and also movie writer. He recollected his student days and wrote about Venkataramaiah :-

Muchukota Venkata Ramaiah garu is the father of my good friend, Chandra Sekhar. He was also the respected teacher for both of us.

In those good old days, two schools were very well known in Kurnool, one being the Coles Memorial High School and the other, the Municipal High School. There was an intense rivalry between the students of these two schools - particularly in the sports arena. Whenever there was a match between these two teams, atmosphere became so surcharged, as if India and pakisthan teams were playing. Chandrasekhar and I studied in both these schools.

The memorable experiences are varied and many. I have studied sixth class in Cole's Memorial High School. The then Head Master was Babu Rao, a close friend of my father. Venkata Ramaiah was our Telugu teacher. Even to-day, I clearly remember the songs he made us to sing, than the text book lessons he taught us.

There was a big shady tree near the school compound. The students sat under the tree. Venkata Ramaiah's standard dress was a light grey coloured long coat, white dhothi and a turban. He was the personification of dignity and simplicity. While he sang meaningful, moralistic and patriotic songs, we followed him. One song in particular which helped to mould my attitude and personality, still echoes in my ears and vibrates on my tongue. (song in telugu script is given in Annexure - 3D)

"Kulamu Matha Sankuchitha bhaavamu lalama neeyaka maanasammuna
kalalu gaanchina swargakhandamu gaaga Bharatha Boomi jeyaga
Bhaaratheeya kumaara veera prathina gaikonaraa"

Freely translated theessance ofthesong is:-

"Let not the narrow passions of caste, creed or religion engulf your psyche,

Strive hard to make our mother land a "Dream Come True!"

And take a vow to that effect, O Son of India !'

The influence of this song has made me cut short my name, so that no hint of any caste is apparent.

But sadly, the present social trend is to add caste prefixes or suffixes to one's name, even by those with whom it was not an usual practice earlier.

I fervently hope that there should be more and more committed teachers like Venkatramaiah garu, so that the student community will be more enlightened.

In Kurnool, our house was in Kothapeta. I remember, "ANDHRA GRANDHALAYAM", the reputed library founded by Venkata Ramaiah, was located in the neighbouring Narsimharaopeta. Venkata Ramaiah sought neither any Government support nor any private donations to run the library. What is more, he sold away his own properties, as and when needed, for the library's sake. It was a laudable 'One Man Show' indeed!

People called him 'GRANDHALAYAM THATHAIAH' (Grand Paa of the library), with affection, admiration and awe!

I always remember our respected teacher, Sri Muchukota Venkata Ramaiah garu, the Grand Old Man of the library movement, with reverence."

K.Hampaiah ,Retired Mandal Education Officer Gadwal:*He was a student of Coles Memorial School from 1948 to1952. His education was in Kannada medium before joining Coles Memorial School . While correcting his composition book Venkataramaiah could understand his deficiency in reading and writing Telugu. He asked him to come to Andhra Granthalayam, gave him small books and guided him to overcome his difficulty. Hampaiah became proficient in Telugu in a matter of six months. He recollects the tips Venkataramaiah was giving to remember important events in history. He found that Venkataramaiah experienced rest in work,looked upon work as worship. Venkataramaiah had self less unconditional love for the students. His teaching as scout master inspired devotion for service.*

R.Daniel Sadhu, Headmaster(Retd) Rockwood School, Kurnool: *Venkataramaiah had dignified appearance. He taught us drawing. On entering the class he walked to the black board, took thick threads from his pocket. He used to smear the threads with chalk.*

Holding the threads tactfully and patting with duster he made impressions of grid lines with suitable scale on board and completed the figure. Students were advised to modify scale to suit their books. He recollects the punctuality and regularity of Venkataramaiah and adds that his discipline, honesty were appreciated by correspondents like Prof. Rockwood, Mr. F.G.Christenson and Dr.T.G. Gipson.

P. Ramsingh, Mandal development officer (retired) narrated an experience. *He studied in Coles Memorial High School from 1952 to 1956 classes 9th to S.S.L.C (11th class). Every student was permitted to take two books from library per week. Ramsingh collected two books. Even before he came to the recording table Venkataramaiah informed that the book was read by him a month earlier which was a fact. He was astonished at the memory of the teacher.*

Students appreciated explanation and tips to remember Telugu grammar and verses. His emphasis was to make students understand that Telugu verses were designed for easy memory. Only requirement was they should be read with proper division of words.

Retirement of Venkataramaiah and felicitation by teachers :- Teacher's of Coles Memorial HighSchool honoured Venkataramaiah at the time of his retiremen with the title "vangmayodharaka"

A few verses were composed in Telugu in praise of Venkataramaiah at the time of retirement. Translated summary is presented here under:-

The Lord (Vishnu) created a universal stage for the enactment of great play (world) as composed by Goddess Saraswathi, the goddess of knowledge. He created a son (brahma) who is awesomely adorned by her. That Lord shall give you long life "O" Sir Venkataramaiah. You have received highest education available here.

On completing your college education, you returned to this school and served for 37 years. Every one praised your services. Apart from this you have established a library. It is difficult to describe your greatness. We definitely are not praising to please you. Your dress depicts Andhra culture. Your dealings depict devotion. You always tried to help others. You never get tired in your work. Thus you are the embodiment of qualities of a good teacher.

Inspired by the way you taught English, Telugu and Art,

Your devotion to work obedience to administration and friendly disposition are admired.

Having recognized the noble and hidden urge for human development, sustained activity for many years to promote Scout activity,

Pleased with your service, the head of the high school, at the time of your retirement honoured you with presenting a gift of one hundred and sixteen rupees.

We do not have the intention of bidding farewell to you. But it is inevitable. Our affection towards you can never get diminished as you are bestowed with great wisdom. "O" Sir Venkataramaiah, You are admired by people; you are a great teacher, "Vangmayodharaka". (One who greatly uplifted literature.)

The verses are composed by D. Narasimha Sarma. (The verses in telugu script are given as Annexure - 3E)

One of his students Ramana Gowd painted his portrait and presented it to the school. Venkataramaiah was in the habit of composing verses and songs to teach, patriotism. good habits and life history of patriots. At the time of his retirement he handed over manuscripts to be kept in school library. One manuscript with titles Seethamma Dandakam (Garland in praise of Seethamma) Seethamma Vinuthi (song requesting Goddess Seetha) available in Telugu script is given as Annexure - 3B, 3C.

CHAPTER - 12

VENKATARAMAIAH AFTER RETIREMENT

After retirement Venkataramaiah confined himself to the library and house. He was in the habit of getting up at 4 A.M. After initial routine he used to sing Ranganadha Ramayana. He was gifted with sweet voice. His voice used to reach three to four neighbouring houses. He was performing Sandhyavandanam thrice a day. His house gave shelter to volunteers of library movement and adult education when they were on tour to Kurnool town. Venkataramaiah almost led a monotonous life. He did not spend even a single evening for entertainment. He never attended any function in the evening even if it was at Kurnool.

Holi festival was celebrated in Narasimharaopet in Karnataka style. The children went round the houses singing songs to collect unserviceable furniture, fire wood andeverything that could be burnt. Before lighting the pyre which is a token of burning Manmadha by Lord Shiva, Children approached Venkataramaiah for a sketch depicting the incident. He used to draw the sketch in a matter of minutes. Children watched with pleasure the outline and strokes with pencil to complete the drawing. The sketch used to be placed on the pyre and burnt.

Dr.D.S. Reddy vice chancellor Osmania University (1957 to 1969) was a childhood friend of Venkataramaiah. He was a native of Cheemalavaagupalli which is about 10Kms from Muchukota. During 1961 he visited Venkataramaiah after a gap of 30 years. Dr.Reddy evinced interest to know about the status of libraries in Andhra Pradesh. Venkataramaiah tried to understand changes in educational policies of government. Only a few reminiscences of childhood and youth transpired during talks.

Glow in the eyes of Venkataramaiah and overwhelming joy appeared during their meeting.

Many students were discontinuing studies as they could not pay fees. If any student approached Venkataramaiah, he paid the fees.The only thing the student had to do was to attend to the repair of some damaged books. He always advocated the principle of dignity of labour.

The report on 36th annual celebration of Andhra Grandhalayam was given in monthly magazine Granthalaya sarvasvam. The translated extract is presented hereunder

GRANDHALAYA SARVASVAM :-

Annual Function *:- The Andhra Grandhalayam of Kurnool celebrated its 36th anniversary on Saturday, 2 Aug 1958 at 5 PM. Janab Mahaboob Ali Khan M.L.A.of Kurnool presided over the function and S.Narayanareddy Muncipal Chairman Kurnool was also present.*

After the customary prayer, students participated in recitation competition of hymns and verses of 'Srimad Bhagavatam' and the winners were given prizes by the chief guest. In the function, D.V Narasimha Sharma brought out to every one's notice that Smt.Venkamma sister of Venkataramaiah had contributed immensely for the 'Grandhalaya Udyamam' by supporting her brother financially and by managing the lands near Muchukota village. Her demise was deeply regretted by him.

Retd. Municipal High School Head Master K.N Pasupati, B.A,LT., spoke about the history of the Library at length. He praised M Venkata Ramaiah on his work and promised to contribute material worth Rs 1,000 to the Library.

Janab Mahaboob Ali Khan then brought out that Andhra Grandhalayam was not only a matter of pride for Kurnool but to the entire Rayalaseema region. He promised to do his best in assisting the Library. He praised Sri M. Venkata Ramaiah for his great work and wished him good health. The function ended with the National Anthem.

Andhra Pradesh Granthalaya Samstha District units were formed during the year 1959 under the chairmanship of Pathuri Nagabhushanam,Secretary Andhra Pradesh Granthalaya Samstha. A meeting was convened in Andhra Granthalayam Kurnool on 29-11-1959 to form the Kurnool district body. Venkataramaiah was elected as member and continued to contribute for improvement of libraries in the district. Even after enactment of A.P. Library legislation he served as member of Kurnool forum.

In the year 1965 the 41st annual function of Andhra Granthalayam was celebrated. D.Narsimha Sarma, teacher, Coles Memorial High School, read out a few verses extempore summary of which is as follows;-

Andhra Granthalayam is temple established to make citizens of Kurnool fortunate.

"Vangmayodharaka" Venkataramaiah is a punctual priest. Readers seeking knowledge are identified as devotees. The annual functions are compared to functions organized by God Brahma popularly known as Brahmosthavalu.

He desired that by grace of Goddess of knowledge, Saraswathi, the Andhra Grandhalayam should develop eternally consuming sacred waters of Thungabhadra and knowledge acquired by readers as fruits.(Verses in Telugu are given in Annexure - 3F).

K.Rosaiah, Secretary(retired)Andhra Pradesh Grandhalaya Samstha, wrote his reminiscences for the book Granthalayam Thathaiah. He mentioned that he had an opportunity to meet famous leaders and volunteers of library movement and devoted officials of various libraries. In his vast experience he had not seen one who ran library as one man show without taking government assistance for such long period of fifty years.

On attaining the age of sixty five.the eyesight of Venkataramaiah diminished. He used hand lens to read.

As children grew, with inflation and increase of needs, expenditure increased many fold. Retired from service he was only dependent on income from lands. Coles High School was a private school as such he was not entitled to pension. Change in the attitude of tenants with social and economic changes reduced the income from lands. Death of his sister Sindhiraju Venkamma, who stayed at Muchukota and was mainly responsible for collection of rents further reduced his income. Selling of lands became inevitable.

CHAPTER - 13

PARADOXES IN LIBRARY MOVEMENT

After independence some founders of private libraries approached the government and obtained funds maintained them and after the formation of state libraries they were handed over to the government.

As time passed many social, political and economic changes took place. Sri.Pathuri Nagabhushanam famous library movement leader in editorial 4-1959 of "Granthalayasarvaswam" described the situation of library movement in Telugu translation of which is as follows:

Now Andhra library movement is in a paradoxical stage. When we were under foreign rule, the rulers were against spreading education lest it should jeopardize their very existence. They viewed every social welfare activity with suspicion. Library movement was not favoured by rulers. Many intelligent and devoted volunteers came forward and stood with commitment to fulfil their duty towards the nation. Their efforts resulted in successful implementation of library movement from from beginning of 20th century till the achievement of independence in 1947. The movement along with development of language induced national spirit and also economic and social awareness. The movement got support only from self inspired citizens and was highly successful and spread through out the country.

After independence a great change occurred in the perception of citizens. They lost interest in the institutions they established, strived for their sustenance and growth. They began to perceive that government should take the responsibility of the institutions.

Government could not do justice to the institutions because of innumerable obligations. Many programs were stalled for want of funds. Institutions and establishments of Library movement suffered most. The library acts were passed by the government to reduce the burden on inputs by voluntary organizations to establish and maintain libraries. When funds were not released in time or were insufficient, volunteers wanted to reduce their burden by shifting burden to government institutions. Thus overall progress in this sphere got hampered."

From1960 onwards paper became freely available. Cheap paper served many magazines to last only for a specific period. Cost of printing got reduced. Abundant variety of books of all categories got published to suit various types of readers. Libraries which could generate income and become source of livelihood for many youth emerged. They are popularly known as rent a book libraries. They survived only for some years. Television changed the scene and is mainly responsible for closure of rent a book libraries.

In the libraries of higher educational institutions teaching staff select the books.

Students' representatives in selection committee improve selection. In the state library authority institutions, selection committees prescribe the list of books which can be procured.The committee in Andhrapradesh functions under Director of libraries who does not have experience of maintaining any sort of library even for a single day. He does not haveknowledge of common reader. In most cases readers will not have a say, interests of common man rarely gets represented. Representatives of members of libraries and readers may improve quality of books procured. Only a person with degree on library science and expierience of maintaining libraries should be posted as Director of Libraries.

Venkataramaiah was in the habit of procuring books requisitioned by the readers in general and the scholars in particular who visited library.Perceptable change occurred in type of books required by readers.

Importance of recitation diminished with analytical education methods and instruments based on them. Verses which promote easy recitation lost importance. Prominence of Telugu classical literature got subdued with questioning their validity. It is felt that teachings in them cannot be practiced in fast moving modern world. People preferred simple and easy language. Spoken language books got preference. They reflected day to day life. Literature Arts and History got lesser priority over science and professional subjects.Basic sciences also lost importance. Cost of classics and other thought provoking books remained above the affordability of common man. Interested readers can only look to good libraries. Some old classics, epics and other philosophical books are being made available at affordable prices by religious institutions. Philanthropists contribute to make them affordable to common man.

CHAPTER - 14

TRIBUTES FOR SERVICES RENDERED TO LIBRARY MOVEMENT

After independence aspiring volunteers of library movement engaged themselves in various developmental activities, politics and other activities required for development of the nation. Some of them entered education field. Very few remained in library activities. Those that were young and fit for absorption in government libraries were absorbed. Rest of those interested in libraries was permitted to join service and they were appointed on acquiring requisite qualifications. Very few still continued with the libraries established which survived with individual or society efforts. By 1972 the number of such libraries was so small as twenty one in Andhra Pradesh. Many volunteers in their old age realised that memories of leaders and volunteers of library movement who sacrificed the comforts of family life and properties were being lost and so they collected information of volunteers and tried to record them. This process was initiated only after about 30 years of Independence. Most reminiscences were lost.

Efforts of Dr. Velaga Venkatappaiah in this direction are commendable. Sri Mahalakshmi Enterprises Vijayawada published a book with the title "Jeevitha Charitra kosam of Granthalaya Karyakarthalu" is edited by Dr. Velaga Venkatappiah.In this book efforts of 100 leaders and volunteers directly connected with Libray Movement and110 leaders and volunteers that were active in other movements,and still contributed significantly to library Movement are presented. In pages 163 to165 brief report on the efforts of Venkataramaiah is given. (Annexure - 2)

Edire Chennakesavulu collected Information about Venkataramaiah. Edire Chennakesavulu, a resident of Hyderabad was associated with Khadi movement. He was a follower of Vinobha Bhave popular freedom fighter, Organiser of bhoodhan movement.

Dr. Velaga Venkatappaiah wrote another book with the title "Granthalayasevanirthulu". He included information about many librarians also In this book.

He listed donations given to libraries in the form of properties in Andhra Pradesh. Details are as follows:-

DONORS WHO DONATED TO LIBRARIES / LIBRARY MAINTANANCE AS IF IT WERE THEIR OWN KIN

1) *Sri Uttakuri Subbaraya Shetty, Vetapalem, Prakasam Dist. Donation : His own house and 5 acres of land for Saaraswatha Niketanam.*

2) *Sri Bhupati Raju Tirupati Raju, Kumuvalli, W.Godavari Dist., Donation : 5 acres of land for Poet Vireshalinga Library.*

3) *Sri Komma Sita Raaamaiah, Patamatalanka, Vijayawada. Donation : 6 acres of land for AP Library Association.*

4) *Sri Verapalli Venkata Reddy, Potavaram, Prakasam Dist. Donation : 2 acres of land for Village Library.*

5) ***Sri M. Venkata Ramaiah and Smt. Sindiraju Venkamma, Kurnool. Donation : 20 acres of land and 10 acres of land for Andhra Grandhalayam, Kurnool respectively.***

6) *Sri Shanivarapu Subba Rao, when offered a house by Desodharaka Kasinathuni Nageswara Rao Pantulu garu for his residence as he was not in possession of one, refused the house for himself and requested him to offer the house for his Library.*

Thus Venkataramaiah was one of the six persons committed to the library movement who considered library to be one of their children and distributed property.

Andhra Granthalayam served society for 50 years before and after independence.

This library's name found place in the book which listed important libraries in india. The following is the extract.

MEN OF LIBRARY SCIENCE & LIBRARIES IN INDIA

Edited by : ***RAJ K. KHOSLA***

Associate Editor : ***M.K. GAUR***

1967

PREMIER PUBLISHERS (INDIA),

POST BOX 2578, 9/6601,

DEV NAGAR, KAROL BAGH, NEW DELHI - 5

STATE & PUBLIC LIBRARIES,

ANDHRA PRADEHSH

Andhra Grandhalayam, Kurnool : 7(1)

ANDHRA GRANDHALAYAM, KURNOOL (A.P.)

Founded in 1923, the Library is being managed by a private body. The library practices closed access system and provides facilities to the public. Classification is done subject – wise and Alphabetical and Classified Catalogues are maintained in Manuscript form. The Library remained closed for 182 days in the year

Coverage : Literary and General Subjects.

Sri Venkataramaiah's continued effort and devotion towards library movement attracted the attention of publishers who gave a gist of his achievements along with his photo as detailed here under:-

DIRECTORY OF BOOKSELLERS PUBLISHERS

LIBRARIES & LIBRARIANS IN INDIA

(Who's Who) Edited by

RAJ K. KHOSLA

1968-69

PREMIER PUBLISHERS (INDIA)

P.B. 2578, F-117 SUDARSHAN PARK,

NEW DELHI – 15

VENKATARAMAIAH. M;

Manager and Librarian Andhra Grandhalayam, Kurnool; *b* 5 Oct 1894, Distt Anantapur;

Edn Trained Teacher, Scout & Drawing Master Madras Univ; *Exp* Teacher-cum- Asst Librarian Coles High Schl, Kurnool 1918-55, *Hobb* Book mending & binding ; *Add* Manager, The Andhra Grandhalayam, 43-93- N.R.Pet, Kurnool (A.P.)

GOLDEN JUBILEE FUNCTION (1919-1969)

The golden jublee celebrations of Andhrapradesh library association were held during the last week of Dec' 1969 at Tirupathi. The report of the proceedings published in "Granthalya Pragathi" Volume IV. Translated extract is presented hereunder

Andhra Pardesh Library Association GOLDEN JUBLEE function was conducted from 27th to 30th December 1969 in Sri Venkateswara University presided by Dr. G. Chenna Reddy. University Telugu Reader Sri T. Kodanda Ramaiah inaugurated Grandhalayam Association's book "Grandhalaya Pragathi" and brought out its special features. Dr. G. Chenna Reddy informed that since ages Libraries have been integral part of healthy societies and only by extensive reading of various books alone help development of humanqualities to the end. We can republish books like "Appakaviyam".

On this occasion Andhra Pardesh Library Association President Sri Ayyanki Venkata Ramanaiah felicitated the following who actively participated in Library movement-

(1) Civil Libraries Ex- Director Sri Raghava Reddy.

(2) Cuddapah District Library Association Chairman Sri R. Ranganatham.

(3) Nellore Social Library's Librarian Sri M.V. Subba Rao.

(4) Andhra Grandhalayam Manager Sri M. VenkataRamaiah from Kurnool.

CHAPTER - 15

DEMISE OF VENKATARAMAIAH

Sri Venkataramaiah suffered hip fracture during February 1970. He fell down from a table while he was placing books in specified racks. He could recover and the library continued to serve the needs of society with the help of his elder son M.V. Chalapathy. Venkataramaiah suffered another fall during July 1971. His movements got restricted to the house. Occasionally he used to sit in the library. Dr. Thilak, Dr.R.J. Sreenivas, and Dr. Krishna murthy Naik attended on him with affection. Age took hold of him.He remained in bed from January 1972. His soul left his body on 4-4-1972.

Grandhalayasarvaswam recorded his demise in the following manner in telugu which is translated.

Sep 1972 Demise of Founder of Andhra Grandhalayam

We regret the sad demise of founder of one of the famous libraries of Andhra Pradesh 'Andhra Grandhalayam' Sri M. Venkata Ramaiah on 4 April 1972. He had dedicated his life for his Library which happens to occupy more than three quarters of his own house and he had arranged certain amount of his property for the purpose of maintenance of the Library. He is a great example for many and his life has been self less. May God Almighty bless his soul with peace and happiness. We extend our condolences to his family.

Venkataramaiah's eldest son M.V.Chalapathy continued the maintenance of Andhra Granthalayam with the help of nephew Y. Sreenivasarao till June 1979. Family financial position did not permit the continuation of library.

Government of Andhrapradesh in G.O.MS.No.766 Education (E) Department. Dt.19-7-78 Constituted a committee with the following members.

1) Vavilala Gopalakrishnaiah,Sattenapalli, Chairman
2) Sri Kodati NaryanaRao. President, Andhrapradesh Library Association, Member.
3) M.BhojiReddy, City Granthalaya Samstha, Hyderabad, Member.
4) Director of Public Libraries Convenor.

The following were the terms and conditions of the committee :-

i) To review role played by private libraries to render library service,
ii) To suggest measures as to how best private libraries can help iln the cause of library movement,
iii) To identify good private libraries in the state,
iv) To evolve a system of grants in aid to private libraries for their promotion and
v) To submit its report to government with in a month from the date of its constitution.

Subsequently the term of the committee had been extended up to 17-11-1979. in Government Memo No.2273-E1/78-1 Education Dt.18-8-1978.

The Committee visited the following Libraries:

1) Raja Raja Narendra Andhra Bhasha Nilayam, Warangal 2) Vysya Grandhalayam, Warangal 3) Vasavi Grandhalayam, Warangal.4) Saraswathi Jyothi Grandhalayam, Karim Nagar 5) Bapuji Vachanalayam, Nizamabad 6) Saraswathi Grandhalayam, Visakhapatnam 7) Sarada Grandhalayam, Anakapally 8) Gouri Grandhalayam, Anakapally 9) Gouthami Grandhalayam, Rajahmundry 10) Sri Velidandla Hanumantha Raya Grandhalayam, Vijayawada.

11) Rama Mohana Free Library & Reading Room, Vijayawada 12) Vasavi Grandhalayam, Vijayawada 13) Ganesh Steel Traders Library, Samarangam Chowk, Vijayawada 14) Tikkana Grandhalayam, Guntur 15) Arya Vysya Yuvajana Grandhalayam, Ongole 16) Saraswathi Nekethanam, Vetapalem ***17) Andhra Grandhalayam, Kurnool*** *18) Vysya Mitra Grandhalayam, Narasaraopet 19) Progressive Union Library, Nellore 20) Tribal Library, Nellore 21) Sri Krishna Devaraya Andhra Bhasha Nilayam, Hyderabad 22) Marathi Granth Sangrahalaya, Sultan Bazar, Hyderabad 23) Shoeb Memorial Library, New Malakpet, Hyderabad 24) Bharat Guna Vardhak Samastha, Shalibanda, Hyderabad.*

The committee visited Andhra Granthalayam Kurnool on 23-10-1978. Recommendations of the Committee are as followed.

After visiting the libraries we are convinced that these and other private libraries continue to sustain entirely on the enthusiasm and determined work of local enthusiasts and that finance is their major constraint. To enable libraries to discharge variety of responsibilities discussed in the previous chapter. They have to receive adequate support, financial and otherwise, since their exsisting resources are meager.

Venkataramaiah's family was not in a position to receive help and to continue Andhra Granthalayam. The Library was closed in June 1979.

CHAPTER - 16

CONCLUSION

Venkataramaiah acted as per his aspiration and so led a life of satisfaction. He chose his path at an early age and never deviated from it. God gave him necessary fortune which he utilised generously for the good cause he selected. He wanted to spread education in a complex society that posed numerous limitations. The subjects had restricted freedom, suffered from acute poverty because of British Rule. They were divided because of caste system. Illiteracy multiplied their problems. Venkataramaiah never wanted to be a social reformer or place himself in position that attracts undue attention. He wanted to serve the society in a manner that suited him and his status.

In initial stages he received expert advice. Prof. B.J. Rockwood gave required guidance. He recognized the urge in Venkataramaiah, gave shape to his ideas, first appointed him as teacher allowed him to acquire required qualifications later. He lent his support in equipping Andhra Granthalayam initially with books. He was responsible for developing Andhra Granthalayam on scientific lines.

Support given by O. Lakshmana Swamy Bar-at-Law, the then Chairman Kurnool Municipality further encouraged Venkataramaiah. Leaders like Gadicherla Harisarvotham Rao,Ayyanki Venkataramaiah Maharaja of Kalahasthi Raja Rama Rayaningar enhanced his interest.

Most of the visionaries in those days felt that independence was the main aim and assumed that all problems would be solved thereafter as there would be no exploitation due to foreign rule.

Venkataramaiah continued his mission and did not stop his work even after Independence. Kodati NarayanaRao, Pathuri Naga Bhushanam and many others associated with Venkataramaiah in continuing the movement supported each other in days neglected by the Government. They are responsible for the present library system which could not be further refined because of changes brought in by development. Dr.Velaga Venkatappaiah's contribution towards keeping the reminiscences of great volunteers' of library movement alive need to be appreciated.

Dr. K. Sivbhushanam Professor (Retired) Kurnool Medical college, a scholar in Telugu and English is closely associated with Venkataramaiah's family as a neighbour. His description of Venkataramaiah is as follows :

" Who would not adore or like Venkataramaiah?

His simplicity his foresight and above all his high sense of devotion to humanity cannot but appeal to every one.

A man of simple living and high thinking he elicited admiration even from his worst enemies.

Dressed in khadi dhothi along with a sella, a trift of hair on back of his head he always resembled a mini Gandhi.

Wedded to movement of extension and expansion and spread of knowledge, he really justified his existence in this mundane world."

ANNEXURE - 1

1) Andhra Valmiki Vavilakolanu Subbarao (1863 - 1939)

He is a great devotee of Sri. Rama. He resigned to his job as Telugu pandit Christian college Madras spent rest of his life at the famous Ontimitta Temple in Cuddapah district. All the property he had was given to the Temple. He collected donations and renovated the temple. His translation of Ramayana into Telugu is popular.

2) Chief Minister of Madras state Panuganti Venkatarama Rayaningar (1866 - 1928) :-

Kalahasthi zamindar. Chief Minister of Madras during 1921-1926. Great scholar. Founder of Indian school of medicine and is responsible for formation of Andhra University, a great Patron of Sanskrit learning and a first batch postgraduate from Christian college Madras.

3) S.M.Foosil :-

He was the Secretary Madras Library Association.

4) Sri. Ayyanki Venkataramanaiah (1888 - 1979) :-

Prominent leader of library movement leader. He was influenced by Bipin Chandrapal. He entered public life in 1907 and was instrumental in establishing the first state library association in India, Andhradesa Library association in1914. He also participated in the formation of Library associations in many other states. It is not anexaggeration if one says that he toured almost all villages in Andhrapradesh. He founded library journals like Andhrabharathi (1910), Grandhalaya Sarwaswam (1916) Indian Library journal 1924. He is honoured with title "Granthalaya Pithamaha". Government of India honoured him with Padmashree award.

5) Gadicherla Harisarvothama Rao (1883 - 1960) :-

Popularly known as Andhra Tilak. Closely associated with library movement and adult education. Member of legislative council (1927-1930). Worked as the editor of 'Swarajya, AndhraPatrika, Mathruseva,The Nationalist, The Grampanchayathi, The Andhravartha, Grandhalaya Sarwaswam and The South Indian Adult Education review'. He was arrested during vandematharam movement and undergone regerious imprisonment.

ANNEXURE - 2

The work carried out by Venkataramaiah as presented by Edire Chennekesavulu, volunteer of Sarvodaya movement in Telugu is translated and is as follows (Pages 163 - 165) :-

Muchukota Venkata Ramaiah (1894) He was born in Muchukota village of Anantapur District. His father Venkatarayudu was Karanam of the village. He completed his Primary education at Thadilpatri, Middle school education at Anantapur, and High School education at Kurnool, and intermediate education at Madras. He saw the drama "Droupathi vasthrapaharanam" as child. He procured at first prose version of Adiparvam and later all 18 Parvas of Maha Bharatham. A constable residing in the village paid two anas per month and read all parvas paying two anas per month. As a boy he was reading Mahabharatha for his grandmother. At that age he was not in a position to understand completely the verses. He was approaching the learned as he grew old for the meaning and interpretation of the verses. This enabled him to develop interest in mother tongue. He started buying books and read dramas, novels and other literature.

He wanted to extend the benefit of reading to others that had interest to pursue knowledge. He started a library in Kothapeta locality of Kurnool town with forty books. Initially he was lending books free of cost. Readers mis utilised the facility. He started collecting deposit and monthly subscription. Initially he prepared and passed Karanam test. He joined as a clerck in taluk office Thadipatri and worked for a period of six months with a salary of twenty rupees per month. Later he joined as a teacher in Coles Memorial High School where he had his High School education. He served for thirty eight years and retired. He was appreciated by students and colleagues. During 1958 teacher's community conducted farewell function and awarded the title 'Vangmayodharaka' meaning enhancer of literature.

He served for six years as member of local library authority and conducted meetings in various villages of Adoni, Aluru, Allagadda taluks encouraged locals to establish libraries. He served as president of Kurnool forum of Andhrapradesh library association for a period of three years.

The AndhraGranthalayam he established and maintained occupied three fourth of his house. There are about seven thousand books belonging to different disciplines. Most of them are Telugu books. Next to Telugu there are books in English apart from a few Hindi and Urdu books. Most of the books are procured by Venkataramaiah with his own funds. He subscribes for many important telugu magazines, children literature and attracts specially children. Subscribers are fifty in number. He does not seek Government aid lest it should hinder his freedom. He made arrangements for continuation of library by his successors with the income from his gift of twenty acres of land and his sister.

Smt. Sindhiraju Venkamma gave a gift of ten acres of land. From the beginning he personal did all the work related to library. He gave librarian training to his sons venkatachalapathy and Chandrasekhar and hoped that they would continue the library after him. His wife Smt. Adilakshmidevi assisted Venkataramaiah in all his endeavours treating guests and visitors with due respect. Venkataramaiah did not establish library to be praised by others. However many naturally praised his efforts. Important persons that praised his efforts include Andhra Valmeeki Vavikolanu Subbarao, Chief Minister of Madras State Panuganti Raja Rama Rayanin garu, Secratary of Madras Library Association S.M.Foosil, Prominent leader of Andhra library movement Ayyanki Venkataramanaiah and Popular freedom fighter Gadicherla Harisarvothamarao.

ANNEXURE - 3A

శ్రీరామ శతకము

శ్రీ వేంకటరామయ్య గారు **1910**లో రచించిన శ్రీరామ శతకము వారికి గల ఆంధ్ర భాషాభిమానాన్ని తెలుపుతుంది. శతకం లోని మొదటి పేజి ఈ క్రింది విధంగా ప్రచురితమైనది.

శ్రీరస్తు

శ్రీరామచంద్ర వరప్రసాదలబ్ధ కవిత్వమహత్వ యశోవిరాజితార్వేలకుల కశాబ్ధిమధ్యస్థిత
భట్టర్‌వంశాఖ్యశ్వేతద్వీపాంతర కల్పవృక్షాయమాన వెంకటరాయామాత్య గర్భపుష్పసంజనిత ఫలోపమ
సకలసజ్జన విధేయ వేంకటరామనామధేయ కవివర ప్రణీతంబున

శ్రీరామ శతకము

ఇయ్యది

శ్రీమద్రామభద్ర విధృమారుణమృదుచరణ సంసేవామహత్వసంలబ్ధాదితాంధ్రకవిత్వ విద్యాద్వితీయ
వాగ్వైభవ సమన్వితాఖిల విద్వజ్జవవిధేయ భీమ రాజాస్వయాంభోనిధి రాజనారాయణ రాజాత్మజుండును
చంద్రహాసాభ్యుధయాది గ్రంథవిరచతానంత కుశలుండును అమ్మళ్ళదిన్నె ప్రథమ పాఠశాలోపాధ్యాయుండును
నగు బి.ఓబళరాజనామ కవివర్యునిచే సరిచూడబడి వరదాయపుర నివాసుల ధనసహాయముచే మదరాస్
బరూరు త్యాగరాయశాస్త్రులవారి గీర్వాణభాషారత్నాకర ముద్రాక్షరశాలయందు ముద్రింపబడియె.**1910**

శ్రీకరమగులోకేశుడ
ప్రాకటముగనాత్మలోనబ్రార్థించియుమి
మ్మేకమనంబునవేడెద
మీ కరుణతో బ్రోవవయ్యమేదినిరామా 1

వాసవముఖదివిజులచే
భాసురముగపొగడ బడినభవ్యాత్మకనే
భూసురుడను త్రిగుణాత్మక
వాసిగనార్వేలవాడ వరగుణరామా 2

కరివరద ముచ్చుకోటను
పురమున రామయ్యయనెడిపుణ్యాత్మునకున్
నరవందితనేమనుమడ
ధరవేంకటరాయునకును దనయుడరామా 3

వరధీరజనావనయో
సురసేవితదివ్యపురుషశుభకరనామా
హరనుత కాశ్యపగోత్రుడ
ధరవేంకటరామయాఖ్యదనరితిరామా 4

క్షితిలక్షణగ్రంధంబుల
వెతకియునేజదువలేదు విపులముగాగన్
కృతిచేయగ మొదలెతెలియదు
సతతముమిముగొల్చువాడసద్గుణరామా 5

మీదయ గల్గుట చేతను
నే దీనిని కవిత జేసి నిశ్చల బుద్ధిన్
శ్రీధర యర్పణజేసితి
యేదోషములున్ననీవేయినకులరామా 6

కమలజు వేదములను గొని
యమరంగా సోమకుండు యబ్ధినిదూరన్
సమరంబుజేసి వానిని
సమయించినమత్స్యరూప శాశ్వతరామా 7

వారాశియందు దివిజులు
కోరిక గిరి నునిచి దరువ కుంగుచునదియున్
నీరధి మునుగగ కూర్మమ
వై రయముననిల్చినట్టి యచ్యుత రామా 8

భీకరుడు హిరణ్యాక్షుడు
లోకంబుల బాధజేసి లోకాధిపతిన్
వీకతో గూల్చెదననగా
సూకరమైద్రుంచినట్టి శుభకర రామా 9

హరు వేడమన్న బుత్రుడు
హరినేదలచంగ దండ్రి హామిక చేతన్
బరిపరిబాధల బెట్టగ
నరహరివై దనుజు ద్రుంచు నగధరరామా 10

ఇల మూడడుగులదానము
నెలమితొాగైకొనియు నంతనిందద్రుడుమెచ్చన్
సులభత పాతాళమునకు
బలినణచిన వామనుడవు భవహర రామా 11

పగ దీర్చుటకై భూమిని
నగరంబుల వెదకి మనుజనాధులవరుసన్
పగటున గీటడగించిన
భృగురాముడవీవెకావె భీషణరామా 12

దివిజులు మొరలిడగను విని
భువిలో దశరధునకగ్ర బుత్రుడవగుచున్
రవికులమునందు బొడముచు
వివరముగను రాక్ష సేంద్రు విరచిన రామా 13

ఇలలో బౌద్ధుడవైమరి
బలరాముండ నెడిపేర బద్మాక్షునకున్
ఎలిమితో భ్రాతన బరగిన
బలవంతుడవీవుగావె భవ్యుడరామా 14

ధరలో దుష్టుల బాధకు
కరివర దాతాళ లేము కావుమటంచున్
సురలటువేడగ చెడుగుల
కరమొప్పుగద్రుంచినట్టి కల్కివి రామా 15

ఘనమునియైన వసిష్ఠుడు
దనరుచు శాస్త్రంబులెల్లదప్పకదెలుపన్
ఆనువుగదెలసిననినునే
వినుతించగ నెంతవాడవీరుడరామా 16

భవతీ భిక్షంబిమ్మన
నవరత్నలాదిగాగ నగలనునివ్వన్
అవి యెల్ల దెచ్చిగురునకు
సవినయముగనొసగినట్టి సద్గుణరామా 17

చనువుగ విశ్వామిత్రుని
వెనువెంటంజనియు నధిక వీరత్వమునన్
గినుకను మారీచాదుల
ఘనముగ నోడించిక్రతువుగాచినరామా 18

వాటమగు నిశితశరమును
సూటిగ కోదండమునను శూరతమెరయన్
పాటిగ నెక్కిడివేగమె
తాటకిధర గూల్చినట్టి దశరధరామా 19

ఆనువుగ శబరీనతినతి
వనఫలములదెచ్చియిచ్చి వరమిమ్మనుచున్
దనరుచువేడినస్వర్గము
ఘనమతితోనొసగినట్టి ఘనుడవురామా 20

సరవితో విశ్వామిత్రుడు
వరుణాస్త్రము మొదలుగాగ వరశస్త్రములన్
వరదుడమీకైయొసగగ
సరవితొగైకొన్నధీర సాహసరామా 21

భువిపాలు రెందరో
శివుచాపంబెత్తలేకసిగ్గునబోవన్
ఆవలీలనెత్తిదానిని
జవమొప్పగ దృంచినట్టిజానకిరామా 22

జనకుడు సంతోషంబున
దనపుత్రినిసీతనివ్వ దద్దయుప్రీతిన్
మునిజనములు దీవించగ
ననువుగ బెండ్లాడినట్టి యచ్యుతరామా 23

జనకుని యానతి మీరక
వనములకున్ బోవుచుండ వచ్చెదమనుచున్
అనుజుడు సతియునువేడగ
కనికరమున నొప్పుకొన్న ఘనుడవురామా 24

అనుజుడు దెలియక రాక్షస
మునినొక ఖడ్గంబుచేతమోదగనటకున్
మనమున రేగుచువచ్చిన
దనుజు దునుమాడినట్టి ధైర్యుడరామా 25

లంకాధీశుండీసున
పంకజముఖి నేవుమేర బట్టణమునకున్
బింకముతో గొని పోవుట
పొంకముతోదెలిసిగొన్న పుణ్యుడ రామా 26

ఇన సుతుడగు సుగ్రీవుడు
మనమున సంతోషమొంది మైత్రినిసల్పన్
ఘనముగ వాలిని గూల్చెద
నని యభయం బొసగినట్టి యనఘుడరామా 27

అంగుష్ఠముచే దుందుభి
భంగపుకాయంబు వేగబహుదూరముగా
చెంగున నెగరంజిమ్మిన
సంగరభీషణుడత్యసంహ్మారరామా 28

ఇనసుతుడు జూచుచుండగ
ఘనకార్ముకమెక్కుబెట్టి గాంభీర్యమునన్
అనువుగ తాళంబులవడి
దనరుచుభువిగూల్చినట్టిధశరధరామా 29

జలజాప్తసుతుడు వాలియు
చలమునుబోరాడుచుండసాహసమతివై
బలురయమున నొకశరమున
నిలవాలినిదృంచినట్టి యినకులరామా 30

అభిచరులతోసుగ్రీవుని
యభిరామంబైనపురికి నరిగియునచట
అభిషిక్తుడవైరమ్మని
యభిమతమున సెలవొసంగు యచ్యుతరామా 31

ఇనపుత్రుడు హనుమంతుని
దనరుచుజానకిని వెదుక దక్షిణదిశకున్
బనుపుచునుండగ ముద్రిక
నెనరుననిడినట్టి కమలనేత్రుడరామా 32

హనుమంతుడులంకకుజని
యనువుగ తావచ్చినతెర గాద్యంతముగన్
ఘనముగ జెప్పగ వినియును
మనముననుప్పొంగినట్టి మాన్యుడరామా 33

శరణని రావణుతమ్ముడు
సరగుననీమరుగుచేర సాహసమొప్పన్
కరుణతొబ్రోచినధీరుడ
నరసురనుత పరమపురుష నగధరరామా 34

తనరుచు విభీషణునకును
ననువుగ వనచరులుమెచ్చ నభిషేకంబున్
మనమున జెలగుచు లంకను
ఘనముగనొనరించినట్టి ఘనుడవు రామా 35

జలనిధి తెరువీకుండిన
బలుకోపమునొందియంత బ్రహ్మాస్త్రంబున్
జలమటు నింకుటకొరకై
పొలుపారిగదొడగినట్టిపూజ్యుడ రామా 36

అచ్చెరువొందగరావణు
జెచ్చెరఘనతూపులేసి జెలగుచువానిన్
అచ్చుగ లంకకుసురలటు
మెచ్చగనురికించినట్టి మేటివిరామా 37

దండిగధనువును దాల్చియు
మెండగు కాండంబులేసి మేటులకెల్లన్
గుండెలురుఝల్లన దైత్యుల
చెండాడిన వవీధైర్యశ్రేష్ఠుడరామా 38

అమరారుల బలుదురమున
సమయించగవలెనటంచు శస్త్రాస్త్రములన్
మమతతో రథమున నింద్రుడు
బ్రమదంబున బనుపగొనిన బద్రుడరామా 39

దురమునరావణు శిరములు
మరికరములుదృంచ నవియు మగుడన్ బుట్టన్
ఆరయుచు విస్మయమొందిన
ధరణీవర భక్తవరదదశరధరామా 40

దనుజేంద్రు నమృతకలశము
ననలాస్త్రంబేసిదాని నార్చియుయంతన్
దునియలుగ కరశిరమ్ములు
ఘనముగధరగూల్చినట్టి ఘనుడవురామా 41

భువనంబులన్ని యొక్కట
కవళంబుగ జేసిమ్రింగ గలిగెడు దైత్యున్
అవలీల ధరణిగూల్చిన
నవసుందరనిర్మలాత్మ నయగుణరామా 42

సురసిద్ధసాధ్య గణములు
అరదుగ జయజయ మటంచు ననుచుండగ
దురమున రావణుధ్వంచిన
దరధరవరవీర ధైర్యదర్పితరామా 43

భువనంబులన్ని యొక్కట
భువిజనములుదలచిముక్తి బందుదురనుచున్
దివిజేంద్రునిచేనెంతయు
బవరముగా బగడబడినభాసురరామా 44

కమలభవాండము నేలెడి
విమలుండవు సర్వవేద విదుడవుననుచున్
అమరులునందరుగూడగ
కమలుజుచేవేడబడినగౌరవరామా 45

సరవితోరావణుధ్వంచియు
సురలనుపోషించునట్టిశూరుడవరయన్
దురమునధీరుడవీవని
హరుచేస్తుతియించబడినయచ్యుతరామా 46

అనువుగసీతాసతితో
నెనయుచు పష్పకవిమానమెక్కియువీకన్
వనచరవరులనుగూడుక
ఘనముగపురి జేరనరగు ఘనుడవురామా 47

మనమున హర్షమునొందుచు
జనుచుండగనపుడువరుసజరిగినపనులన్
జనకునిపుత్రికివినుమని
దనరారుచుదెల్పినట్టిదశరథరామా 48

నందిగ్రామమునకుము
న్ముందుగ జనివార్తలెల్లమోదముభరతున్
జెందగ దెల్పుమటంచును
నందముగా హనుమబనుచు నతిబలరామా 49

సరవితోనయోధ్యకునుజని
శిరులప్పగభూసురాభిషిక్తుడవగుచున్
ధరపతులకువనచరులకు
వరభూషణలొసగినట్టివంద్యుడరామా 50

పరమానందము జెందుచు
భరతుప్రార్థించమిమ్ము పౌరులుమెచ్చన్
వరభూషణాంబరాదుల
సరగున ధరియించినట్టి సాహసరామా 51

వనచరులను హనుమంతుని
యినపుత్రుని యంగదాది యిష్టులవరుసన్
దనరుచుపురములుజేరగ
వినయంబునబనిచినట్టి వీరుడరామా 52

వాసిగ తమ్ములుగొల్వగ
భాసితమగు ధరనయోధ్యపౌరులు మెచ్చన్
ఆసక్తి మీరజేకొని
భాసురముగ నేలినట్టి భవ్యుడరామా 53

విముఖుడు గార్గ్యుడు కణ్వుడు
సముఖుడు జాబాలికాది సన్ముని ముఖ్యుల్
సుమహితమతి కుంభజుతో
నమరగరాబూజలొసగుయచ్యుతరామా 54

దనుజేంద్రుని వృత్తాంతము
దనరుచుమునిపుంగవుండుదడయక దెలుపన్
ఘనముగదెలసిన ధీరుడ
జనవందితనిర్మలాత్మ జానకిరామా 55

జనకునికైవడి మిమ్ముల
జననాథుడనమ్మినాను చయ్యనమీరున్
జనుడనిభూషణలసగియు
జనకునిపురి కనచినట్టి జానకిరామా 56

ధనపతి బ్రీతివిమానము
దనరుచుబనుపంగనతగి దానితోమరలన్
జనమెట కైనదలంచిన
ఘనముగరమ్మన్నయట్టి ఘనుడవురామా 57

అరుదుగ పురోపవనికిని
సరసముగా సీతతోడ సంతసమొదవన్
వరరథమెక్కుచుజనియును
సరసోక్తులజెలగినట్టి సాహసరామా 58

నిమినృగురాజులకథనం
బమరంగానీశుచరిత్ర మంతయు వరుసన్
అమలతలక్ష్మణవినుమని
రమణీయముగాగదెల్పురఘుకులరామా 59

ఆవిరళబలు శత్రుఘ్నుని
చ్యవనాదిమహర్షులెల్లచయ్యనవేడన్
లవణాసురడను దుష్టుని
బవరంబున ధ్వంపుమనుచు బనచినరామా 60

మునియనబరగిన శూద్రుని
ఘనఖడ్గము దాల్చివాని ఖండించివెసన్
దనరుచుభూసురపుత్రుని
ననవుగ బ్రతికించి నట్టి యనఘరామా 61

ఘనహయ మేధముజూడగ
జని లక్ష్మణసకలమునుల చయ్యన నిటకున్
వినయమునదోడితెమ్మని
దనరారుచుబనచినట్టిధరణీరామా 62

మునివరులందరురాగా
వినయంబునమ్రొక్కివారి వేడుచుగడకన్
ఘనహయ మేధముజేయగ
ననుమతి గైకొన్న రాక్షసాంతకరామా 63

వనచరులను ధరపతులను
ఘనమునమనబంధువులను గ్రక్కుననిటకున్
ననువుగదోడుకరమ్మని
యొనరగలక్ష్మణునకాజ్ఞనొసగినరామా 64

మరిగోమతీతీరంబున
సరగున మఖశాలయొకటిచయ్యనపుడున్
వరశిల్పులబిలిపించియు
ధరమెచ్చగగట్టమన్న దశరథరామా 65

పురజనులభూసురుల
వరభటులను నాశ్రితులను వంద్యుల మరియున్
సరగున వీణావాద్యుల
భరతుని రప్పింపుమని బనిచిన రామా 66

ఇనవంశోద్భవుడగునా
యనుజన్ముడు లక్ష్మణుండు యశ్వంబునకున్
అనువుగ రక్షకుగనిలిపి
ఘనహయముకు ఫాలముననుగట్టినరామా 67

బలవంతులుగా నుండిన
బలుమరునివ్వాజిగట్టి పట్టుడులేదా
వలసినయాభరణాదుల
సలలితముగ నొసగుడన్నసాహసరామా 68

జనులందరు కీర్తింపగ
మునులందరు త్రుప్తినొందిమోదముజెందన్
అనువుగ హయమేధంబును
ఘనముగ ముగియించినట్టి ఘనుడవురామా 69

పదిలముగాగ నయోధ్యను
సదయుడవైయందు జనులు సంతసమొందన్
పదునొక్కవేలయేడులు
వదలక పాలించినట్టివంద్యుడరామా 70

భవదీయంబగు నామము
భవహరమని నమ్మినేనుభక్తితోనెపుడున్
అవనీశదలంచుచుండెద
నవసుందరనిర్మలాత్మనయగుణరామా 71

శరణనివేడినవారల
సరవితోరక్షించు సాహసమొప్పన్
వరదుడమీకుంగలిగెను
సురసేవిత భక్తవరదశోభితరామా 72

ఏవపుజన్నము ధరలో
భూవరనేజెంద వెంచి బూజ్యడమిమ్మున్
కావుమనిశరణుజొచ్చితి
పావనినుతనన్నుబ్రోవుభవ్యుడరామా 73

తల్లివి తండ్రివినీవని
యుల్లంబునదలచి నేనునొప్పుగ మిమ్మున్
ఎల్లప్పుడువేడెదనభూ
వల్లభనను కరుణజూడు వరగుణరామా 74

ఈవనయము నాతప్పుల
కావవెమిముదలచినేనుఘనముగ నెపుడున్
భావనజేసెదమదిలో
భావనగుణకరుణజూడుపట్టపురామా 75

కరుణతొభక్తులబ్రోచిన
వరదుడవీవనుచు దెలసి వర్యుడనాకున్
ఆరుదుగనాశలుబుట్టెను
దిరముగ నాతాపములనుదీర్చవరామా 76

దురహంకారుడగావున
సురసేవితనాశ్రయంబుజొచ్చితిమిమ్మున్
సరగునసద్గుణమిచ్చియు
నరవంద్యుడనన్నుబ్రోవు నగ ధరరామా 77

దాసుడమీకని మనవిని
జేసితినను పాలనంబుజేయవె మరియున్
గాసిలియుంటిని రాఘవ
దోసిలి బట్టితిని బ్రోవు దోర్బలరామా 78

దీనశరణ్యుడకృపమీ
వానిగ నన్నేలుకొనవె వాంఛలుదీరన్
మానుగనెప్పుడు మదిలో
ధ్యానమునే జేయుచుందు దప్పనురామా 79

పట్టితి తమ పాదంబుల
గట్టితి తమ దాస్యమునకుగంకణమిపుడున్
నెట్టవె దోషంబులనె
ప్పట్టున ననుగావవయ్య బల్మరురామా 80

న్యాయము జెందగ మరిన
న్యాయముమదిజేరకుండ నచ్యుతనన్నున్
బాయకయుండెడిప్రభువీ
వేయనినినునమ్మినాడనిప్పుడురామా 81

ఎక్కడజూచిన భువిలో
నక్కజముగ నీదుమహిమ లంతటవెలసెన్
జక్కగవేడెద రాఘవ
మక్కువ నాపైనయుంచుమాన్యుడరామా 82

నిను గొనియాడెదశ్రీధర
ఘనముగ మీపైనభక్తిగలుగగనిమ్మో
సనకసనందన వందిత
యనువుగ మిము దలచుచుందునచ్యుతరామా 83

అపదలు బాయజేయవె
నీపదముల నమ్మి నేడు నిశ్చలబుద్ధిన్
తాపములన్నియు విడచియు
ప్రాపని నినుజేరినాడ భరమారామా 84

శాంతగుణంబులచే భూ
కాంతుడ నాకోర్కెలెల్ల గడతేర్చవెనిన్
స్వాంతములోదలచుచు న
త్యంతము మరివేడుచునుందుననఘుడరామా 85

తనరుచు నుండెదవంతట
ఘనరూపుడ నిన్ను నేను గనుగొనజాలన్
అనువుగనీమాయలనే
వినుతించగనెంతవాడ వీరుడరామా 86

చక్కని నీరూపంబును
మక్కువతో సాకుజూపు మాన్యుడమిమ్మున్
పెక్కువిధంబులవేడుచు
జక్కగనేమ్రొక్కులిడుచుశాశ్వతరామా 87

తప్పులనెంచక రాఘవ
ఒప్పుగ నను మీదు కడను యుండెడినటులన్
తప్పకవరమిమ్మనినే
నెప్పుడు మిము గోరుచుందు నినకులరామా 88

వింటిని మీ కథలను మరి
గంటినిమీ పాదములను ఘనుడానేమీ
వెంటం దిరుగుచునుండెద
బంటుగ నన్నునేలవయ్య భవ్యుడరామా 89

స్రుక్కెను నాపాపంబులు
దక్కెనుతమపాదసేవధరణీస్థలిలో
చిక్కెనిదే మీ కథామృత
మక్కజము జుర్రుకొందునాశనురామా 90

సతతము మీపాదపద్మము
అతిభక్తితోబూజజేసి యచ్యుతమిమ్మున్
మతిలోదలచుటకంటెను
యితరంబేనొల్లనైతినినకులరామా 91

చల్లని చూపుల చేతను
నెల్ల సుఖంబుల నొసగి యెప్పుడు సీతా
వల్లభననుబ్రోవవెనా
యుల్లంబుననమ్మినాడ నోపికరామా 92

చక్కెరయు క్షీరంబును
నక్కజమగుఘృతముమరియునన్నిటకన్నన్
ఎక్కువరుచి మీనామమె
యెక్కడనుండిననుదలతు యినకులరామా 93

అమితములగుపాపంబుల
కుమతినినైజేసినాడ గొంటెతనమునన్
ఆమరగ పరిహారమునకై
అమలుడ నిను వేడుచుందునచ్యుతరామా 94

ఇనవంశుడ లోకేశుడ
జననుతడాభక్తవరద సారెకుమదిలో
ఘనబలుడవునీవనుచును
దనరుచునేదలచుచుందు దశరథరామా 95

అమితదయారసుడవుస
ద్విమలుండవు పరమపురుష వీరుడవరయన్
సమధిక గుణుడవుననిమీ
సముఖంబునుజేరినాడ సాహసరామా 96

ఏమివరంబనివేడుదు
నామదిలోకోర్కెలెన్నోనగధరగలిగెన్
భూమిజనాథుడయిప్పుడు
నీమముతోనిన్నుగొలుతు నిర్మలరామా 97

నమ్మియుమీచరణంబుల
నెమ్మనమునదలచుచుందునెనరునదేవా
నెమ్మతమగు శ్రీమోక్షము
నెమ్మితోనాకొసగువయ్య నేర్పునరామా 98

ఒప్పులతప్పుల నెరుగను
జెప్పితినేనేర్చినట్లు శ్రీకర మీరున్
ఒప్పుగనా మనవిని నే
చొప్పునగైకొంద్రొతెలియశోభితరామా 99

మంగళము భానువంశజ
మంగళము దయాబ్ధి సాంద్రమంగళమెపుడున్
మంగళము సకలరక్షక
మంగళమిదెభక్తవరద మనుకులరామా 100

శ్రీ రామార్పణమస్తు

ANNEXURE - 3B

శ్రీ సీతమ్మ దండకం

1. శ్రీ మన్మహాదేవి నీరేజ పత్రేక్షణా
2. కుంద కల్హార, చాంపేయ, సౌగంధికా
3. పుష్ప ధమ్మిల్ల సంకాశ భాసమానా
4. చిత్ర కస్తూరి,రేఖాంచితా, మంద
5. హాసా, మహా పద్మ రేఖాన్వితా దివ్య
6. తాటంక సంపూర్ణ రత్న ప్రభాజాల
7. గండస్థలీ మంజువాగ్వైఖరీ నిత్యసం
8. తోష భక్తావళీలోల సంరక్షణా
9. చిత్త భాసాపరంజ్యోతి రూపీ మహా
10. దైత్య భూతాది భేతాళ వర్గాది
11. సంహార శక్తి త్రినేత్రీ త్రిరూప మహా
12. మంత్ర యంత్ర ప్రశస్తాధికారీ
13. జగన్మోహినీ దేవతా పద్మపాణీ రమా
14. వైభవానంద శృంగారగాత్రీ మహాఘోర
15. సంసార తాపత్రయా భీల పాపంబు
17. లన్ నీదు నామంబుచే మాయమైపోవు
18. నీ పంచ భూతంబులున్ వృద్ధిగా జెంద
19. నీయందు బద్నాల్గు లోకంబులన్
20. జంద్ర సూర్యాదులు న్నష్టదిక్పాలకుల్
21. యక్ష గంధర్వ సిద్ధుల్మహాదేవ సం
22. ఘంబులున్ శైలముల్ దివ్య రత్నంబులున్
23. గల్గు మాయా ప్రపంచంబు మాయంబుగా
24. జేయు భూతేశ్వరీ సర్వ సంపత్కరీ
25. సర్వ లోకక్రియాశక్తివైయుందువే
26. నీవు నిర్మింపగా బ్రహ్మయుంగూడి యి
27. ఛ్ఛాప్రకారంబుగా సర్వవేదంబులున్
28. సర్వ మంత్రంబులున్ సర్వతంత్రంబులున్
29. పద్యము ల్గద్యముల్ కూడి యా
30. త్మసంభూతమై తోచి ప్రజ్ఞానశక్తి
31. రమాదేవియై విష్ణుతో గూడి భోగార్హ
33. నాద బిందు స్వరూపాక్షరా హంసతత్వం
34. బుతో మూడు వర్ణంబులై యేకమై
35. దివ్యమై సేవ్యమై భవ్యమై దివ్యతేజో నిరా
36. కారమై సర్వసాక్షి ప్రసన్నంబు లోలాడు
37. భద్రేభయానా మహామోహపాశంబులన్
38. గట్టు నీ శక్తిచే మత్త శుండాల ముల్బైంధ
39. వానీకమున్ ఛత్రము ల్భిన్యముల్గల్గు
40. కారుణ్య సంపత్తిచే నిత్య కల్యాణీ
41. సీతా మహాదేవీ శ్రీరామభద్రుండు
42. వైకుంఠవాసుండు నీవే మహాలక్ష్మీ
43. మీ కన్న నింకేమియున్ లేదు మిమ్మున్ సదా
44. స్తోత్రముల్సేయు పుణ్యాత్ములున్
45. దివ్యులై వచ్చి సారూప్య సాయుజ్యముల్బొంద
46. రే దీన మందార వృక్షా స్పదాహేతు చి
47. త్తాన్వితా యెంచ శేషాహికైనన్ వశంబౌనే
48. శ్రీ రామదేవీ నమస్తే నమస్తే నమః

ANNEXURE - 3C

సీతమ్మ వినుతి

జననీ సర్వం సహాదేవి జనకుడఖిల
శాస్త్ర గుప్తార్థ సిద్ధుండును సజ్జనాభి
రాము రాత్మే శ్వరుండుగ రాణమిగలు
అర్థి జన కల్పవల్లి సీతమ్మ తల్లి

విప్రరసనాగ్ర మంజుల వేదఘోష
యు జనకరాజు పొందిన యజ్ఞఫలము
తరణికులము వెల్గించు రత్నాల దివ్వె
అర్థి జన కల్పవల్లి సీతమ్మ తల్లి

సంశ్రిత జనాఘ కార్పాస సప్తజిహ్వ
విశ్వ కారణు బ్రకటించు, వేదబుక్కు
హరి పరంజ్యోతి దెల్పునధ్యాత్మవిద్య
అర్థి జన కల్పవల్లి సీతమ్మ తల్లి

విమల దుగ్ధాబ్ధి దేటిన యమృతరసము
హరి యురము వన్నెపెట్టుననర్ఘ భూషణ
ఆగమాంతర్నిహిత పరమార్థ చయము
అర్థి జన కల్పవల్లి సీతమ్మ తల్లి

ధర్మపత్నీత్వ లబ్ధికాదర్శరేఖ
శ్రీరఘూద్వహ హృదయ దయారసంబు
మదిని సత్రి గృహిణి మెచ్చుమణిశలాక
అర్థి జన కల్పవల్లి సీతమ్మ తల్లి

పుణ్యజనయోషి దవన కారుణ్యరాశి
గర్భమున జంటముత్యాలగన్న శుక్తి
యాద్యకవి మంత్రపరిపాకమైన కరుణ
అర్థి జన కల్పవల్లి సీతమ్మ తల్లి

మహిత గార్హ స్థ్య ధర్మప్రమాణ పంక్తి
పవనతనయ సుదృక్పుణ్య వర్ధనంబు
హుత వహుడు సోకవెరచినయుజ్జ్వలాంగి
అర్థి జన కల్పవల్లి సీతమ్మ తల్లి

ANNEXURE - 3D

మైనంపాటి భాస్కర్‌ను ప్రభావితం చేసిన పాట

కులము మత సంకుచిత భావము
లలమనీయక మానసమ్మున
కలలు గాంచిన స్వర్గఖండము గాగ
భరతభూమి జేయగ
భారతీయ కుమార వీర ప్రతినగైకొనరా

దీని గురించి పేజి నం. 61 లో ప్రస్తావించబడినది.

ANNEXURE - 3E

శ్రీ కర్నూలు ఆంధ్రగ్రంధాలయము 41వ వార్షికోత్సవ సంధర్భమున

సీ// కర్నూలు పౌర భాగ్య స్థాపితాంధ్రగ్రం
ధాలయ మొక్క దేవాలయముగ
స్థాపక వాఙ్మయోద్ధారక వేంకట
రామయ్యనియతినర్చకుడుగాగ
వాసిగ పిపాసచేనరుదెంచు
పాఠకావళిభక్తపాలుగాగ
నేటేట జరిపెడి నీ వార్షికోత్సవాల్
క్రమమగు బ్రహ్మోత్సవములుగాగ

గీ// ప్రధితమౌ తుంగభద్ర తీర్థంబు గాగ
ప్రాజ్ఞ విజ్ఞానమే మంచిఫలముగాగ
ధరణి వర్ధిల్లు నాచంద్రతారకముగ
దివ్యవాణీ కృపారస దృష్టిబలిమి.

ANNEXURE - 3F

ఆదర్శతపస్వి శ్రీవాఙ్మయోద్ధారక యం. వేంకటరామయ్య గారికి ఉద్యోగవిరమణ సందర్భమున వీడ్కోలు.

శా॥ శ్రీ వాణీనట నాగ్రరంగముగ నోలిన్ లోకముంజేసి వా
ణినిస్రంభ విశేషపాత్ర మగువానిన్ బుత్రుఁగామన్ని వా
గ్దేవి౯ రంజిలఁజేయుస్రష్ట విధిగాదీర్ఘాయు రారోగ్య ర
క్షావిఖ్యాతులోసంగి ప్రోచుతను వేంకట్రామ యార్యా! మిమ్ము

ఉ॥ చాలుగ నిందు నున్నతపుఁ జద్వుముగించియు లీలగాఁగళా
శాలను మెట్టివచ్చి యిటఁ జక్కని యొజ్జగ ముప్ప దేడు వ
ర్షాలుగ నుండి యందఱి ప్రశంసలనందితి రింతెగాక గ్రం
థాలయ మొండు నిల్పితి రహో! భవదున్నతి నెన్న శక్యమా!

ఉ॥ ఖాయముగా పఠింతుము ముఖస్తుతి గాదిది, కార్యదీక్ష, య
న్యాయము లేని వృత్తి మనయాంధ్రతఁ జాటెడు వేషభాషలున్
సాయమునేయు శీలమల సత్త్వ మెఱుంగని యత్న మిట్లు పా
ధ్యాయ గుణంబులెల్లఁ దమయందె వసించెను సద్గురూ త్తమా!

సీ॥ ఆంధ్రాంగ్ల చిత్రకళాది పాఠావళి
బోధనశక్తి కుప్పొంగి యేమొ!
ప్రభుభక్తి, స్వవిధి నిర్వహణ, వత్సలతాది
సుగుణంబులకుఁ గడుఁజొక్కి యేమొ!
మానవాభ్యుదయ నిదాన సత్ప్రకల
క్షణపూర్ణ తను గాంచి తనిసి యేమొ!
బహువర్షకృత బాలభట సంఘ నిస్తుల కార్యకలాపంబుఁగాంచి
యేమొ!

కే॥గీ॥ తమరు పదవిని విరమించు తరుణ మందు
హర్షి, గిప్సను, పాఠశాలాధినేత
యాంధ్ర మర్యాద నూటు పదార్థ చేత
సత్కరించెను మిము, నెంత సంతసమ్ము !!!

మ॥ మిము వీడ్కో మనసొప్పదైన విధిలేమింజేసి వీడ్కొందు మీ
సమయంబం దయినన్ మమత్వమది యీ షష్టైన లోపింపబో
దు మహా బుద్ధులయందు నెప్పుడు, జనస్తుత్యా! యుపాధ్యాయ స
త్తమ! శ్రీ వేంకటరామ యార్య! నయవిత్తా! వాఙ్మయోద్ధారకా!!!

రచన : విద్వాన్ దేవరకొండ వేంకట నరసింహాశర్మ

ANNEXURE - 3G

పుస్తకాల తాతయ్య

కం. **శ్రీముచ్చుకోట** కులమున
ఏ మచ్చ నెరుగ నంటి నెలబాలుండై
సీమకు మణియగు **వేంకట**
రామయ్య కొసగుచుంటి ప్రస్తుత శతమున్ ॥

కం. గ్రంధ చయంబునకే-సుమ
గంధమ్ము నలందినట్టి కర్మజుండై
గ్రంధాలయోద్యమముతో
భంధమ్ములు పెంచుకొనుచు ప్రధితుండయ్యెన్ ॥

కం. అన్నను తిన్నను నిద్రి
స్తున్నను, కన్నను కథవినుచున్నను నిరతం
బెన్నగ జాలని సేవను
మిన్నగ నుద్యమ మునకిడె మేరునగంబై ॥

కం. అతని పావన జీవన
స్రోతస్విని తెలుగునాట శోభామయమౌ
చేతన కలిగించెడి గతి
నూతనమగు యూతనొసగు నుతు పాత్రంబై ॥

కం. మహితోద్యమమునకు-పితా
మహుడనిబిరుదమ్మునొంది-మాన్యుడటంచున్
విహుతులచే పూజలుగొని-
సహనాత్ముడు ముచ్చుకోట-**శాశ్వతుడయ్యెన్** ॥

కం. పుస్తకముల తాతయ్యా-స
మస్తాంధ్ర వనమ్మున పరిమళములనిదుచున్
మస్తకములందు నిలచుచు
కస్తూరిని పంచుచుండు కాలమ్మెలన్ ॥

పద్యమౌళి, పద్యభాషి
డా॥ రాధాశ్రీ (డా॥ డి.ఎ.వి.ఆర్.కె. ప్రసాద్)
సీనియర్ మేనేజర్, సిండికేట్ బ్యాంక్. సెల్ : 9494481210

ANNEXURE - 4

Copy of Document No.5 of 1904 తాడిపత్రి తాలూకా ముచ్చుకోట గ్రామంలో రామయ్య యింటిలో **1904** వ సం.జూన్ నెల **22** తేదీ పగలు **12** గంటలకు దాఖలు చేసినది. కరణం రామయ్య వ్రాశి ఇచ్చినట్లు ఒప్పుకున్నది (బొటనవేలి గుర్తు) కరణం రామప్ప నల్లప్ప కుమారుడు బ్రాహ్మణ యినాం, ముచ్చుకోట.

నిరూపించినది. **1) V.Hanumantha Rao Son of V. SanjeevaRao Vrahmin. Police Inspector, Tadipatri.**

2) భట్టరు వెంకటనర్సు దత్తు కుమారుడు వేంకటరాయుడు సాక్షి వ్రాలు బ్రాహ్మణ కరణీకం పని వల్ల జీవనం

1904 వ సం.జూన్ నెల**22**తేదీ **K.V.Subbaiah sub registrar.III** పుస్తకం **1**వ వాల్యూం **209-210** ల లో **5** వ నంబరుగా రిజిష్టరు చేయబడినది. **1904** వ సం.జూన్ నెల **22** తేదీ చెల్లించిన రుసుము పద్నాలుగు రూపాయలు.

K.V.Subbaiah sub registrar..

Relavent details 1904 వ సం.జూన్ నెల**22**తేదీలు అనంతపరంజిల్లా తాడిపత్రి తాలూకా సబా తాడిపత్రిలో ఉండే బ్రాహ్మణ స్మార్థ పోలీసు యినస్పెక్టరు పని వల్ల జీవనము చేసే వెలిదిండ్ల హనుమంతరావు గారి కుమారుడు సుబ్రహ్మణ్యం సదరు తాలూకా ముచ్చుకోటలోఉండే బ్రాహ్మణ స్మార్థ కరణీకం యినాం వల్ల జీవనంచేసే కరణం వేంకట్రాయుని కుమారుడు వేంకట్రామయ్య ఈ ఉభయులకు సదరు తాలూకా ముచ్చుకోట గ్రామంలో ఉండే బ్రాహ్మణ స్మార్థ కరణీకం ఇనాం వల్ల జీవనంచేసే కరణం నల్లప్ప కుమారుడు రామయ్య వ్రాయించి యిచ్చి వీలునామా యేమంటే అనంతపురం డికట్టు తాడిపత్రి సబ్ డికట్టు లోచేర్ని ముచ్చుకోటలో గ్రామంలోను భూములు ఇండ్లు,రాయలచెర్వు గ్రామంలోను యాడికి గ్రామంలోను వేములపాడు గ్రామంలోను కోనుప్పలపాడు గ్రామంలోను సదరి అనంతపురం డికటులో చేర్ని అనంతపురం తాలూకా పెరవలి గ్రామంలోను భూములు ఇండ్లు, కర్నూలు డికట్టు పత్తికొండ తాలూకా ప్యాపిలి సబ్ డికట్టు లో చేర్ని బూర్గుల గ్రామంలోను జంబిశెట్టి క్రిష్ణప్ప పేర యినామతి దాఖలా యండి నా స్వాధీననుభవంలో ఉంధే జమీనున్ను యీ ఉదహరించ్చి వుండే గ్రామాలలో నా పేర యినామతి గాను పట్టాగాను ఉండే భూములలో నేను ఇదివరకు యితరులకున్ను మీ తండ్రి గారికిన్ని ఈ దినం సర్కి

విక్రయించి వుండే భూములు తప్ప మిగతా నా తాలూకు యావదాఆస్తులు మీ ఇద్దరు దౌహిత్రులు గనుక నా యొక్కయు నా భార్యయొక్కయు జీవనాంతరము మీరు బాధ్యులయ్యి వుభయిలిద్దరు చేరి అర్ధముగా హక్కు గలిగి అనుభవంచుకోవలశ్నిది.నేను ఇదివరకు ఇచ్చి ఉండే ముని గుత్త కౌళ్ళు జరిపించవలశ్నిదిగానున్నూ నేను నా పెద్దకుమార్తె యీశ్వరమ్మకు లగ్నకాలమందు దానముగా యిచ్చి ముచ్చుకోటగ్రామం పొలంలో సర్వే **333** నంబరు య**1.45**తరము**2-14-0**యీ జమీనుల మీకే వదలవలశ్నది గానున్నూ ముచ్చుకోట గ్రామంలో నేను కట్టించిఉండే రామేశ్వరస్వామిదేవునికిగాను పూజలు జరుపుటకు వుంచ్చి వుండే భూములనగా ముచ్చుకోటగ్రామం పొలంలో సర్వే **168** య **5-3** తరము రూ **10/1/0** సర్వే **177** య **1.6** తరం రూ **3/4/0** సర్వే **14** య**-12.14** తరము రూ **4/9/0** యీజమీనులుకున్ను పైనీ వుదహరించ్చి రాయలచెర్వు గ్రామంలోను యాడికి గ్రామంలోను వేములపాడు గ్రామంలోను కమలపాడు గ్రామంలోను కోనుప్పలపాడు గ్రామంలోను బూర్గుల గ్రామంలోను పిన్నేపల్లి గ్రామంలోను వుండు జమీనులునూన్నూ యివి అన్నీ పైన చెప్పిదేవునికి పూజలు వగైరా జరపుటకు యినాముగా వుంచ్చూతూ జమీనులకు మీరు మేనేజర్లుగా వుండ్డి జరిపించవలశ్నిది. యిందులో ఉదహరించ్చి యేర్పాట్ల ప్రకారము జరిపించుతూ మా జీవనాంత్తరము మీఉభయులు భాధ్యులయ్యి చేరి అర్ధములనుభవింకోవలశ్నిది అని నా మనపూర్వకముగా వ్రాయించ్చియిచ్చి వీలునామా యిందుకు వప్పితమూ కరణంరామయ్య యిందులకు సాక్షులు :

1) అమళ్ళదిన్నె పా.అదినారాయణప్ప/ముచ్చుకోట నర్శిరెడ్డి కుమారుడు బాలిరెడ్డి--సాక్షివాలు.

బిక్కలం పాటిలోరావి కోడయ్య వ్రాశ్నిది.

తుడుపు రిజిష్టరులో హంసపాది వగైరాలులేవు. /c.s.copied by Rangareddy clerk examined byH.Narasimhabutt/K,Subbaiah subregistrar.

ANNEXURE - 5

Relavent details in copy of DOCUMENT No -1024 of 1926 (FILED IN FILE BOOK1 VOL170 pages 146,147)

1000 రూ.లకు భూదాన గృహదాన పత్రము. కర్నూలు జిల్లా కర్నూలు టవును క్రొత్తపేటలో **193** నెం.ఇంటి మేడపైనుండు అంధ్ర గ్రంధాలయము కార్య నిర్వాహకునకు కర్నూలు జిల్లా కర్నూలు టవును క్రొత్తపేటలో నుండు ముచ్చుకోట కరణం వేంకటరాయని కుమారుడగు టీచరు వేంకటరామయ్య వ్రాసి యిచ్చినదాన పత్రము :-

సర్వజనసేవ్యమే యొక సేవనమనియు అట్టి యోక సేవనమే భగవత్సేవయని నాకు ధృడ విశ్వాసము కలుగుటం జేసి ఆంధ్ర భాషాభివృద్ధికిని, జ్ఞానాభివృద్ధికిని తోడ్పడెడు పై గ్రంధాలయమును **1/8/1923** తేదీన స్థాపించితిని. ఈ గ్రంధాలయమును శాశ్వతము గాను అచంద్రతారార్కముగాను నడుపవలెనను ఉద్దేశ్యము కలుగుటచే ఈ గ్రంధాలయ కార్య నిర్వాహతను వంశపారంపర్యముగా నుంచుకొని శ్రీపరమేశ్వర ప్రీత్యర్థంబుగా నీ క్రింది షెడ్యూలులో వివరింపబడిన స్థిరాస్థులను పై గ్రంధాలయ కార్యనిర్వాకునకు అప్పగించితిని. ఈ ఆస్తులను ఆయకముంచుటకు, అమ్ముటకు, కార్యనిర్వాహకునకు అధికారము లేదు. భుములనుండి వచ్చు వరబందిని ఏవిధముగా వినియోగించిన గ్రంధాలయము ఏ వధముగా వ్యయపకుండిన గ్రంధాలయము పనులు జరుగవో అట్టి సందర్భములను గుర్తించి ఆ వరంబడిని వినియోగించుటకు ఈ గ్రంధాలయ కార్యనిర్వాహకునకు అధికారము కలదు. అని నా రాజీనొప్పి వ్రాసి యిచ్చిన దానపత్రము.

షెడ్యూలు

1) కర్నూలు జిల్లా కర్నూలు టవును **41** క్రొత్త పేట వీధిలో **193** నెం ఇంటిపై నుండి **19** అడుగుల పొడవును **13** అడుగుల వెడల్పును తూర్పు వాకిలిని అన్ని దిశలయందును **193** నె యింటిని కల్గిన మేడ

2) కర్నూలు జిల్లా కోయలకుంట్ల తాలూకా కోయలకుంట్ల సబ్ డిస్ట్రిక్టు లో చేరిన చిన్నకొప్పెర్ల గ్రామ పొలములో చేరబడి నా హక్కు అధీన అనుభవములో కల ఇనాము భూముల వివరములు

సంఖ్య	ఖుష్కి ఇనాం	సర్వే నెం.	ఎకరములు /సెంట్లు	రూ. అణాల పైసలు	పేరు	దిశ
1	డి	221 పైకి	2.43	1-3-6	చౌటిచేను 1/2	ఉత్తరము
2	డి	229 పైకి	2.58	5-2-6	నల్లవాగుచేను 1/2	ఉత్తరము
3	డి	241 పైకి	6-47 1/4	12-15-3	చంద్రయ్య చేను 1/4	ఉత్తరము
4	డి	237 పైకి	0.97 1/2	1-15-0	తిరుగు గడ్డ 1/2	తూర్పు
5	డి	235 పైకి	0-13	0-4-0	తిరుగు గడ్డ 1/2	తూర్పు

షరా :- 1 వ నెంబరు లో తెలుపబడిన మేడ 193 నెం. ఇంటి పైనుండుట వలన ఆ ఇంటిలోని వారికి పైన గ్రంథాలయముండుట వలన ఇబ్బంది అని తోచిన పక్షమున అ మేడకు బదులుగా రూ. 500 అక్షరాలా అయిదు వందల రూపాయలకు తక్కువ వెలచేయని వేరొక భవనమును గ్రంథాలయమునకు ఆ ఇంటి వారొసగ గలిగినచో అ ఇంటివారు అ మేడను తీసికొనవచ్చును. ఇందుకు సాక్షులు :-

12-7-1926 M. Venkataramaiah teacher C.M.H school.

B.J. Rockwood Principal Coles Memorial High School.

O. Lakshmanaswamy Bar at Law. Kurnool. 12-7-1926.

బిక్కలం స్వహస్తము వ్రాసినది. ఉత్తరమున రాణోజీ తోటయును తూర్పున పుల్లాజీ ఇల్లును దక్షిణమున హై రోడ్డును పడమట పసుపుల శేషయ్య గారి ఇల్లును ఎల్లలుగా గల 93 నె ఇంటి పైనుండు మేడ.

ANNEXURE - 6

500 రూ.లకు బదలాయింపు దస్తావేజు 1926 వ సంవత్సరం ఆగష్టు నెల 24వ తేదీ కర్నూలు జిల్లా కర్నూలు టవును క్రొత్తపేటలో నుండు అంధ్రగ్రంథాలయము కార్యనిర్వాహకుడగు యం. వేంకటరామయ్య అను నేను (1) సదరు జిల్లా సదరు తాలూకా క్రొత్తపేటలో నుండు ముచ్చుకోట కరణం వేంకటరాయని కుమారుడగు టీచరు వేంకటరామయ్య
(2) అను ఇద్దరము కలిసి వ్రాసుకొన్న బదలాయింపు దస్తావేజు.

ఏ షెడ్యూలులో వివరింపబడి 500 రూ. వెల చేయు పై గ్రంథాలయ ఆస్తిని 2 వ ఇసుమగు యం.వేంకటరామయ్యకు - బి షెడ్యూలులో వివరంపబడి 500 రూ. వెల చేయు 2 వ ఇసుముయొక్క ఆస్తిని సదరీ గ్రంథాలయము కార్యనిర్వాహకుడగు యం.వేంకటరామయ్యకు ఇచ్చుకొన్నాము, కనుక ఇంతటినుండి ఎవరికి ఏ ఆస్తి వచ్చినదో వారు అనుభవించుకోవలసినది.

12-7-1926 వ తేదీన వ్రాయబడి కర్నూలు రిజిష్ట్రరు గారి ఆఫీసులో 1024 నెంబరుగా రిజిష్టరు చేయబడిన దాన దస్తావేజులో ఏ షరత్తులున్నవో ఆ షరత్తులు యిప్పుడు గ్రంథాలయమునకు చెందిన బి షెడ్యూలు లోని ఆస్తులకు అన్వయించును.

షెడ్యూలు ఎ టీచరు ముచ్చుకోట వేంకటరామయ్యకు చేర్చబడిన ఆస్తి కరూలు జిల్లా కర్నూలు టవును 41 నెం. క్రొత్తపేట వీధిలో 193 నెం. గల యింటిపై నుండి 19 అ పొడవు 13 అ వెడల్పును తూర్పు వాకిలిని అన్ని దిశల యందును 193 నెం. కల యింటిని కలిగిన మేడ 193 నెం. గల యింటికి వుత్తరమున రాణోజీ తొటయు తూర్పున పుల్లాజీ ఇల్లును M.Vencataramaiah Manager Andhragranthalayam M.Vencataramaiah teacher C.M.H school ———

దక్షిణమున హైరోడ్డును పడమట పసుపుల శేషయ్య గారి ఇల్లును ఎల్లలుగా గలవు.బి పై ఆంధ్ర గ్రంథాలయమునకు చేర్చబడిన ఆస్తి కర్నూలు డిస్ట్రిక్టు కర్నూలు తాలూకా కర్నూలు సబు డిస్ట్రిక్టులో చేరిన కసబా కర్నూలు క్రొత్తపేట 5 వ నంబరు వార్డు 41 తూర్పు పడమర్లగా నుండే వీధి దక్షిణపు వరుస మధ్య భాగములో నుండి తూర్పు ఈ ఇంటిపైకి శ్రీవేంకటేశ్వరస్వామి వారికి చెందిన యిల్లు దక్షిణము వెంకోజీ అబ్దుల్ రహిమాను అను వారల ఇండ్లు తాలూకు బైలు పశ్చిమము వెంకోజి యింటిలోనికి నవ్వగలందులకై యంటూ యుండే సందు ఉత్తరము రోడ్డు అను చెక్కుబందికి లోనైన తూర్పు పడమర్లు 12 గలూ ఉత్తర దక్షిణాలు 81/2 గలు వస్తీర్ణం కల్గి కప్పు లేక నీటి కొళాయి పాయిఖానా కరివేపాకు చెట్టు కల బయలూన్ను, దీనికి లక్తీగా దక్షిణమున తూర్పు పడమర్లు 14 గలన్ను ఉత్తర దక్షిణము గ 41/2 గలున్ను విస్తీర్ణము కలిగి కప్పుతో నంటూన్న కర్నూలు మునిసిపాలిటీలో 278 నెం. కలిగి ద్వారమునకు ఇరు వైపుల అరుగులు కలిగి కర్నూలు డిస్ట్రిక్టు డోను తాలూకా డోను సబు డి!! లో చేరిన పెండేకల్లు గ్రామస్థులగు బిందుకూరు మామిళ్ళపల్లె అశ్వర్థరామయ్య గారు వారి భార్య రామలక్ష్మమ్మ గారు సర్వ విధములుగా విక్రయమునకు జవాబుదారిగా నుంటూ 21/2/26 వ తేదీన వ్రాయించి 9-3-26 తేదిన కర్నూలు రిజిస్ట్రారు గారి ఆఫీసులో నాకు విక్రయించిన ఇల్లు.

M.Vencataramaiah Manager Andhragranthalayam

M.Vencataramaiah teacher C.M.H school.

Signatures other formalities of registration

ANNEXURE - 7

1200 రూ.లకు విక్రయ దస్తావేజు 1941 వ సంవత్సరము జనవరి నెల 22 వ తేదీలు వ్రాయించు వారు ముచ్చుకోట కరణం వేంకటరాయుని కుమారుడగు యం. వేంకటరామయ్య టీచరు నరసింహరావుపేట కర్నూలు బ్రాహ్మణ కులము వయస్సు 44 సం. వ్రాయించుకొనువారు కార్యనిర్వాహకుడు ఆంధ్రగ్రంథాలయము కర్నూలు. పై గ్రంథాలయమునకు నేను ఇదివరలో ధర్మార్ధముగా ఇచ్చి యుండిన 41 వ నెం. కొత్తపేట వీధిలో 424 నెం. గల ఇల్లు గ్రంథాలయమునకు నిరుపయోగముగా నుండి ఖాళీ నున్నందున సదరు ఇంటి దానమును రద్దుపరచి 1200 రూ. పంన్రెండు నూర్ల రూపాయలకు విక్రయించి సదరు పంన్రెండు నూర్ల రూపాయలకు నా హక్కు అధీనములోనుండు ఈ క్రింది షెడ్యూలులోని భూములను సదరు గ్రంథాలయ కార్య నిర్వాహకునకు విక్రయించి అప్పగించితిని. ఇంతటి నుంచి సదరు భూములను పై గ్రంథాలయ కార్యనిర్వాకుడు గ్రంథాలయ కార్యనిర్వహణము కొరకు సర్వాధికారములతో ఉపయోగించు కొనవచ్చును. నాకు గాని నా వారసులకు గాని ఎలాంటి హక్కు లేదు అని వ్రాసి ఇచ్చిన భూ విక్రయ దస్తావేజుని – **M.Vencataramaiah** .

షెడ్యూలు. కర్నూలు జిల్లా కొవెలకుంట్ల సబు డిస్ట్రిక్టు చిన్నకొప్పెర్ల గ్రామము –

సంఖ్య	ఖుష్కి ఇనాం	సర్వే నెం.	ఎకరములు /సెంట్లు	రూ. అణాల పైసలు	పేరు	దిశ
1	డి	124 పైకి	5.84	11.11.0	రంగప్ప చేను పూరానెంబరులో 1/2	
2	డి	153 పైకి	0.28	0.56	ఆరేమాను చేను 1/2	ఉత్తరము
3	డి	180 పైకి	5.22	10.70	ఆరేమాను చేను	ఉత్తరము
4	డి	181 పైకి	0.33	0.10.6	ఆరేమాను చేను	ఉత్తరము
5	డి	182 పైకి	1.12	2.40	ఆరేమాని చేను	తూర్పు
6	డి	233/1	2.3	2.9	తుమ్మాకుల గడ్డ 12	పంక్తి పై

M.Vencataramaiah.

ANNEXURE - 8

Relavent details Document No 36 of 1941

1941వ సం. జనవరి **7** గృహదానము రద్దు చేయు దస్తావేజు. దస్తావేజు చేయువారు యం. సవేంకటరామయ్య కరణం వేంకటరాయుడు గారి కుమారుడు టీచరు కర్నూలు నరసంహరావుపేట బ్రాహ్మణకులము వయ్యస్సు **44** సంవత్సరములు ఇదివరకు నేను కర్నూలు ఆంధ్రగ్రంధాలయమునకు ధర్మార్థముగా ఇచ్చిన **41** కొత్తపేట వీధి కర్నూలు వుత్తర ద్వారము గల **424** నెం.గల్గి రూ **1000.00** వెల చేయునట్టి ఇల్లు, గ్రంధాలయము పనులకు ఈ క్రింది కారణముల వలన నిరుపయోగముగా నుండి భారముగా నున్నందున సదరు గృహదానమును రద్దు పరచుచున్నాను. సదరు దాన దస్తావేజు రిజిస్టరు ఆఫీసులో **1** వ పుస్తకము **55** వ వాల్యూము **340** పుటలో నెం. **24/1926** రు గా రిజిస్టరయినది.

కారణములు :- నా నివాసము కొత్తపేట నుంచి నరసింహారావు పేటకు మార్చినందున నాకు గాని, నా ఇంటి వారికి గాని గ్రంథాలయము అందుబాటులో లేనందున **2)** గ్రంథాలయము పని జరగని కాలంలో దానిని కాపాడుటకు వాచరు, అందులో కడుగుటకు, శుభ్ర పరుచుటకు స్వీపరు మొదలగు సిబ్బందిని పోషించుటకు గ్రంథాలయమునకు ధనము లేనందున **3)** మున్సిపాలిటి వారు విధించు ఇంటి పన్ను, ట్యాపురేటు పన్ను మొదలగునవి చెల్లించుటకు ధనము లేనందు వలన **4ఎ)** వీధి పిల్లలు గోడపై నుండి బయలులోనికి దిగి ఆటలాడుచూ అల్లరి చేయుచున్నందున **4బి)** కొత్తపేట కంటే నరసింహారావు పేట మిక్కిలి విశాలముగాను, మిక్కిలి ఆరోగ్యకరముగాను, అహ్లాదమగు ప్రదేశం అగుట వలను **4సి)** నరసింహారావు పేట సమీపంలో పాఠశాలలు, బాలుర వసతి గృహములు ఉద్యోగుల నివాసములు మొదలగునవి ఉండి ఉత్కృష్ఠ ప్రదేశముగా వున్నందున **4డి)** కొన్ని వేళలందు వీధి బాలలు బయట ఉన్న కొళాయిని త్రిప్పి నీరు పారించి బురద, న్యూసెన్స్ చేయుచున్నందున **5)** నియమింపబడిన నౌకర్లు వేళకు రాకను వుండవలసినంత సేవ వుండకను, దీపములకు ఇచ్చిన నూనెను తమ పనులకు ఊపయోగించున్నందువలనను **6)** అభివృద్ధి చెందుతున్న గ్రంథాలయమునకు స్థలము చాల నందువలననూ **7)** కాపురం లేని ఇల్లు అయినందున ఇంటి ముందు పెంటకుప్పలు మొదలగునవి పారివేయుచున్నందున **8)** ఎవరికైనను కాపురం ఇచ్చుటకు అందులో వంట ఇల్లు పైఖానా వంటి వసతులు లేనందున ఎవరు బాడుగకు రానందున **9)** ప్రత్యేక గ్రంథాలయ పాలకున్ని నియమించుటకు ద్రవ్యము లేనందున **10)** గ్రంథాలయము పనిచేయు గంటలు సాయంత్రం **5** నుండి **7** గంటలు ఉన్నందున చీకటి కాలమందు, వర్షాకాలమందు అచ్చటి పనులు విచారించుకొని ఇంటికి దూరము నుండి వచ్చుటకు కష్టముగా ఉన్నందునను పై గ్రంథాలయమును నేనున్న ఇంటినే ఉంచుకొనిపై చెప్పబడిన **41/424** గృహదానమును రద్దు పరుచుచున్నాను. పాత నంబరు **4/354.**

ANNEXURE - 9

DOCUMENT No- 828 of 1942 (FILED IN FILE BOOK VOL179)

1942వ సంవత్సరం మే నెల **11**వ తేద్ని కర్నూలు పేటలో ఉండే వయిశ్య కులం వ్యాపారం వల్ల జీవనం చేయు అనంత్త గంట్టయ్య శెట్టి గారి కుమారుడు అనంత్త కొండయ్య శెట్టి గారికి కర్నూలు నరశింహ్వారావుపేటలో యుండే బ్రాహ్మణులు వుద్యోగం వగైరాల వల్ల జీవనంచేయు ముచ్చుకోట వేంకట్రాయుడు గారి కుమారుడు ముచ్చుకోట వేంకట్రామయ్య వ్రాయించి యిచ్చిన గృహ విక్రయపత్రం యేమనగా యీ క్రింది షెడ్యూలులో నమోదించిన యిల్లు కట్టించిన స్థలము నా స్వంత్త ద్రవ్యముతో నేను కొనుగోలు చేసి సదరు స్థలంలో యిల్లు మహడీ వగైరాలు కట్టించినాను. సదరు యిల్లును మీకు రు. **9000.0.0** విక్రయించేందుకు యెర్పాటు చేస్కొని విక్రయించి యున్నాను. నాకు యీ విక్రయ ధనం నాకు ముట్టిన వివరం కర్నూలు గ్రామం శ్రీఅనంత్త నాగన్న శెట్టి గారి పేర నేను వ్రాయించి ఇచ్చిన **43/68** లో యింటి చూపుదాయక పత్రంలో మిగిలిన బాకీ అస్సలు వడ్డి కూడా ఆయకము తీరిపోవునట్లు వారికి మీ వల్ల యిప్పించినవి రు. **2000.** షెడ్యూలు యిల్లు కర్నూలు వకీలు శ్రీ చీరామస్వామి అయ్య గారికి డాక్టరు దీ సంజీవరావు గారి కిన్ని. ఇద్దరి పేరట ఒకటే ఆయక పత్రం వ్రాయించి ఇచ్చి ఆయక పత్రం క్రింద వారికి నేను ఇవ్వవలసిన అస్సలు వడ్డీ రూఢిగా మీరు ఇచ్చినది రు. **4500.0.0.** కర్నూలు గ్రామం బాదం బాలక్రిష్ణయ్య నా పయ్ని కర్నూలు డిస్ట్రిక్టు మునసఫ్ కోర్టులో అప్పీలు నెం. **113 / 1941** గా దావా తెచ్చి సదరు దావాను **22/11/1941** తేద్ని పొంద్ని రాజీనామా డిక్రీ షర్తు మేరకు అతనికి ఇచ్చవలశ్ని రూ.**1370.0.0** అంద్కు అయ్ని వడ్డీ రూ **37-0-0** వెరశి **1407.0.0.** సదరు బాలక్రిష్ణకు మీరు ఇచ్చినద్ని యీ పత్రం రిజిష్టరు కాలంలో శ్రీరిజిష్టరు వారి ఎదుట నేను పుచ్చుకొనబోవునది రూ.**1093.0.0** వెరశి రు. **9000.0.0** అక్షరాల తొమ్మిదినివీ .జవఅఎ్ఘుతీ్ఘఎ్ఘుఋ్ఘుష్ఠ నినివేల రూనినివిక్రయధనం యీ విధముగా పూర్తిగా నాకు మట్టియున్నది గన్క షెడ్యూలు ఇల్లు విక్రయించి యీద్ని కు మీకు స్వాధీనం చేశియున్నాను. యీ యిల్లు కర్నూలో యుండే శ్రీ చీరామస్వామి అయ్య గార్కి దీ సంజీవరావు గార్కి ఆయకం వుంచి యీ యీ విక్రయ ధనములో నుంచి పయికం చెల్లించడము ద్వారా తీరిపోవునట్టి ఆయకంతప్ప సదరు యిల్లు మరి యవర్కి గానీ యే విధమైయ్ని తాకట్టు వుంచలేదనియు వీటియందు నేను వక్కడనే హక్కదారునిగా వున్నాననియు మీకు చెప్పుచూ యీ విక్రయంచేశి యున్నాను. యీ ఆస్తి (టయిటలు) ను గురించ్చి యెవరి వల్లనేగాని యే విధమైన తకరర్లు వచ్చినను అట్టి తకరర్లు నా

స్వంత ద్రవ్యముతో నివర్తి చేయించి యివ్వగలవాడను యే విధమైన తకరర్లు వచ్చిన అందువలన మీకు కలిగే సకల నష్ఠములున్నూ మీరు చేయించి ఉండే రిపేరి ఖర్చులన కట్టకము ఖర్చులున్ను విక్రయధన మున్ను మీకు వాపస్సు యివ్వగలవాడను. యీ యింటి యందు యికమీదట నాకు గాని నా యిలాకా మరియు యవర్కిగాని యలాంటి హక్కులు సంభంధమున్ను లేదు. యింత్తటి నుంచి షెడ్యూలు ఆస్తి మీరున్ను మీ పుత్రులు దానవిక్రయాది వగైరా సంపూర్ణ హక్కులు కలిగి అష్ఠ అయిశ్వర్యములతో సుఖముగా ఆచంద్రార్క స్తాయిగా మీరు అనభవించు కోవలయును అని వప్పి వ్రాయించి యిచ్చిన గృహ విక్రయ పత్రము.

షెడ్యూలు:- కర్నూలు ట కర్నూలు సబ్‌డిలో చేర్నీ కర్నూలు నరశింహరావుపేటలో నేను స్వంత్తముగా **19,20** ప్లాటు స్థలములు కొని, నేను వక్కడనే స్వంత హక్కుతో కట్టించి నా స్వంత హక్కు అనుభవములో యుండే మిద్దె యిల్లు పాతనె **43/78** కోత్త నె **43/91.** యీ యిల్లు యందుకు చెక్కుబందీలు తూర్పు వీ.శ్యామసుందరరావు గారి బయలు జాగా పశ్చిమం సర్కారు రస్తా వుత్తరం సర్కారు రస్తా దక్షిణం కనసరవేసిని సందు రస్తా యీ చతురుదిశలకు లోనయ్ను తూర్పు పశ్చిమం **90** అడుగులు వుత్తర దక్షిణం **60** అడుగులు కొల్తలు గలది. **19** వప్లాటులో కట్టబడియుండే మహడీగల మిద్దెయిల్లు అందులోని రూములు, **20** ప్లాటులో యుండే గాడిఖానా దాని దక్షిణంవుండే రూములు వగైరాలు **19** ప్లాటులోని మహడీమిద్దె యింటికి వుండే తలుపులు ద్వార బందనాలు కిటికీలు యినపదూలాలు, దంత్తెలు అందుగల నివేశం విద్యుచ్ఛక్తి దీపములు వాటి స్విచ్చులు బలుబులు ఇంటికే వేశియుండే సీలింగు ప్యాను ఒకటిన్ని వలువకటి టేబుల్‌ఫాన్ నీళ్ళ కొళయిలు అన్నియు కలిగి వుత్తరం **2** తలవాకిళ్ళు దక్షిణం వక తల వాకిలి గల యిల్లు. యింటిలో బయలు స్థలములు వగైరాలు. యీ యింటికి దక్షణం పడమట వుత్తరం వుండే పూర్తి గోడల హక్కున్ను, తూర్పుతట్టు గోడలో అర్ధం హక్కు గలదు.

రచయిత ముగింపు భావన

తపస్వి వంటి "కీ॥శే॥శ్రీ ముచ్చుకోట వేంకటరామయ్య" గారి సంకల్పం కొనసాగించలేని నిర్భాగ్యులమన్న విమర్శ చాలా కాలంగా ఎదుర్కొన్నాను. మా అన్నగారు యం.వి.చలపతి గారు పెద్దగా చదువుకోలేదు. ఉద్యోగం చేయలేదు. నేనే ఎక్కువ విమర్శలకు గురి చేయబడ్డాను. మా తండ్రి కీ॥శే॥శ్రీ ముచ్చుకోట వేంకటరామయ్య గారిని ఇంత తక్కువ కాలంలోమరచిపోతారు వారిని గురించి వ్రాయవలసిన అవసరం వస్తుందని నేను పదవీ విరమణ 2004 లో చేసిన తరువాత కూడా అనుకోలేదు. కఠిన పరిస్థితులలో మా తండ్రిగారు "పరమాత్ముడు తప్ప ఏది శాశ్వతం కాదు" అని ఊరడించేవారు. ఆ కాలంలో ప్రచారానికి ఆస్కారము ఇచ్చేవారు కాదు. అవకాశాలు కూడా తక్కువ.

1962 లో ఇంజనీరింగ్ కాలేజిలో సీటు పి.యు.సి. మార్కుల ఆధారంగా ఇచ్చేవారు. నాతో సమానంగా మార్కులు వచ్చిన వారికి సీటు వచ్చినా, నాకు రాని కారణం అప్పుడు నాకు తెలియదు. ఒక విశ్వవిద్యాలయ ఉపకులపతి మా తండ్రి రూమ్‌మేట్. మా తండ్రిని బాగా అభిమానించేవారు. ఆకాలంలో ఉపకులపతులకు కొన్ని సీట్లు కేటాయించే స్వతంత్రం ఉండేది. నేను పరిచయం చేసుకొని సీటు అభ్యర్థిస్తానన్నా మా తండ్రిగారు అంగీకరించలేదు. సైన్యంలో పని చేసే మా బావగారి అన్న గారు తను సంరక్షకుడిగా చూపి సీటు ఇప్పిస్తానన్నా ఒప్పుకోలేదు. ఇంకొక్కసారి పి.యు.సి. చదువుతానన్నా సమ్మతించలేదు. "భగవంతుడిచ్చిన దానిని స్వీకరించు, విద్యా విభాగం కంటే చేసే పనిలో త్రికరణ శుద్ధి ముఖ్యం. నిరాడంబర జీవనశైలికి ప్రాధాన్యత ఇచ్చి సంతృప్తితో జీవించాలి" అన్న మా తండ్రి వేదాంతం అర్థమయ్యే వయస్సు కాదు.

ప్రఖ్యాత దర్శకుడు ఎమ్.ఎస్ రెడ్డి గారు ఆత్మకథ రాసి ప్రచురించినారు. 2012లో అది చదివే అవకాశం లభించింది. అందులో విశ్వవిద్యాలయ కులపతి డి.ఎస్.ఎస్. రెడ్డి గారి వ్యవహారశైలిని ప్రస్థావించారు. ముఖ్యమంత్రి నీలం సంజీవరెడ్డి గారి సిఫారసును తిరస్కరించిన నిర్మొహమాటి అని రాసేవారు.

ఉక్రోషంతో ఒక సంవత్సరం బి.యస్.సి. చదివిన తరువాత, కర్నూలులో లేని జియాలజి చదువుతానని మొండికేసి తిరుపతి విశ్వవిద్యాలయ కాలేజీలో చేరినాను. ఆవిధంగా ఇంటికి దూరమైనాను. నా ప్రాప్తం అనుగుణంగా అప్పుడప్పుడే రూపుదిద్దుకుంటున్న భూగర్భ జల శాస్త్ర విభాగంలో చదువు ముగుస్తూనే ఉద్యోగం దొరికి, కర్నూలులో గడపగలిగిన కాలం తగ్గింది. నాకు కర్నూలులో ఒక్కరోజు కూడా ఉద్యోగం చేసే అవకాశం ఇవ్వబడలేదు.

గ్రంథాలయము మూతబడ్డ తరువాత ఒకనాడు అనంతపురం వాసి పోస్టల్ డిపార్ట్‌మెంట్ ఉద్యోగి ఉచిత హోమియోపతి వైద్యం ద్వారా ప్రజా బాహుళ్యానికి సేవ చేసి గౌరవ డాక్టరేట్ పొందిన కీ॥శే॥శ్రీ చలపతిని కలిసి గోడు వెళ్ళబోసుకున్నాను. ఏమీ ఆశించకుండా ఒకరికి ఒక్క రోజు అన్నం పెట్టలేని వారు చాలామంది విమర్శలకు ముందరుంటారు. వారికి సంఘ సేవకుల కుటుంబీకుల కష్టసుఖాలు తెలిసే ఆస్కారం లేదు. బాధపడకు అని ఊరడించారు.

అనివార్యకారణాల వల్ల మా పిల్లవాడు కర్నూలు 1990 లో స్కూలులో చదువుకొనేటప్పుడు మా తండ్రి సమాజసేవను గురించి ప్రస్తావిస్తే "తెరచిన పుస్తకం లాంటి జీవితం గడిపిన, అనితర సాధ్యమైన త్యాగాలు చేసిన మహాత్మాగాంధిని స్వతంత్ర్యం వచ్చే అవకాశం వుందని తెలిసిన నాటి నుండే విమర్శించినారు. కొన్ని వేల సినిమాలు తీసినా మహాత్మాగాంధీని గురించి సినిమా తీసే అవకాశం విదేశస్తుడికే ఇచ్చినారు. మీ తండ్రిగారు చేసిన సేవ, అదీ గ్రంథాలయ సేవను గురించి ఎవరు అనుకుంటారు" అనేవారు.

నాకు నల్లగొండ జిల్లా, మునపటి తుంగతుర్తి తాలూకాలోని నాలుగు మండలాల ప్రత్యేక అధికారిగా (మండలాధ్యక్షులు ఎన్నుకోబడని కారణంగా) 1990 నుండి 1994 వ సంవత్సరం వరకు మా కార్యాలయాధికారి భాధ్యతలు కాక అదనపు బాధ్యతలు నిర్వహించవలసి వచ్చింది. ఆ విధుల్లో భాగంగా అక్షరాస్యతా కార్యక్రమాలను పర్యవేక్షించేవాడిని. నెల దినాలలో అ, ఆ లతో మొదలు పెట్టి చదివి రాయగలిగిన మేధావి వయోజనులను పదుల సంఖ్యలో గుర్తించగలిగినప్పుడు అవకాశం కలిగి వుంటే వీరు గొప్ప వారై వుండేవారనిపించేది. మ తండ్రి గ్రంథాలయములో చదివే చిన్నపిల్లలను గమనించి వారిపై ప్రత్యేక శ్రద్ధ ఎందుకు తీసుకొనేవారో తెలిసివచ్చింది.

లంబాడీ తాండాలు కొన్ని కొన్ని గుడిసెల సమూహాలుగా ఉండేవి. చిన్నదారుల సమూహాలను కలిసేవి. అవకాశమున్నచోట విడివిడిగాను లేనిచోట నేను మండలాధికారులు ఆందరూ కలిసి విద్యాకేంద్రాలను సాయంత్రం గం॥ 6-00 నుండి గం॥ 8-00 వరకు తనిఖీ చేసేవారము. కేంద్ర కార్యకర్తలను, అభ్యాసకులను ఒకసారి అందరు కలిసి మాట్లాడిస్తూ, పురోగతిని సమీక్షిస్తూ సాగేటప్పుడు నాధ్యాసతో నేను సాగిపోయాను. కొంతమంది స్థానికులు నాతో వస్తున్నారు. అరగంట తరువాత అధికారులెవ్వరు నాతో లేరని గమనించి వారెక్కడని స్థానికున్ని ప్రశ్నించాను. ఆయన మీ జీపు ఇక్కడే ఉంది అక్కడ అందరూ ఉంటారులెండి అని జీపు వద్దకు చేర్చాడు.

నక్సలైటు ప్రధాన దళనేత మిమ్మల్ని కొంతసేపు గమనించి వెల్లిపోయారు. మా అదృష్టవశాత్తు వాళ్ళు మీరు సహృదయులని హాని చేసేవారు కారని గుర్తించి వెల్లిపోయారు. వాళ్ళకు అనుమానం కలిగియుంటే మిమ్ములను తీసుకువెళ్ళి వుండేవారు. చాల ఇబ్బంది కలిగేది అని అన్నాడు. 1987 వ సంవత్సరంలో ఎస్.ఆర్. శంకరన్ గారిని కిడ్నాప్ చేశారు.

సాక్షరత కార్యక్రమములో జిల్లాలో మంచి ప్రగతి సాధించిన కారణమున ఆంధ్రప్రదేశ్ రాష్ట్రము తరుపున తమిళనాడులో అక్షరాస్యతా కార్యక్రమాలు జరుగుతున్న పద్ధతి గురించి అవసరమైన మార్పులు సూచించేందుకు నల్లగొండ జిల్లా నుండి ఇద్దరు అధికారులను ఎంపికచేసి పంపించారు. అందులో నేను ఒక్కన్ని.

1995 నుండి 1999 వరకు నోడల్ అధికారిగా మునుపటి మైదుకూరు తాలూకాలోని నాలుగు మండలాలలోని కార్యక్రమాలను పర్యవేక్షించి జిల్లాలో ఉత్తమ నోడల్ ఆఫీసర్‌గా బహుమతి పొందాను. దీనిలో కూడా అక్షరాస్యతా కార్యక్రమ కృషి ప్రధానము. ఈ రెండు గుర్తింపులు నా తండ్రి గారి ఆశీర్వాద ఫలితము.

1994 వ సంవత్సరము నాసహోపాధ్యాయుడు మిత్రుడు అప్పటి గ్రంథాలయ సంస్థ అధ్యక్షులు శ్రీ చంద్రశేఖర్ కల్కూర గారు మా తండ్రి గారి శతజయంతి సంస్మరణార్థం నన్ను పిలిపించి సత్కరించినపుడు నా కుమారునితో ఘనంగా చెప్పకున్నాను.

2003 సంవత్సరంలో ఇటిక్యాల సంజీవరావుగారు, (మున్సిపల్ స్కూలు ఉపాధ్యాయులు, ఐ.సి.యస్.శర్మ గారి పుత్రులు) విశ్రాంత సంచాలకులు ఆంధ్రప్రదేశ్ ఆయుర్వేద విభాగము, డా॥ సుబ్బారావు గారు నిస్వార్థ సేవ చేసిన వారి గురించి ప్రచురిస్తున్నారు. నీవు కూడా మీ తండ్రి వివరాలు ఇవ్వమని కోరినారు. విశ్రాంత కర్నూలు కేంద్ర గ్రంథాలయము కార్యదర్శి శ్రీ కె. రోశయ్యగారు ఇచ్చిన పుస్తకము గ్రంథాలయ సేవానిరతులలో మా తండ్రి గురించిన వివరాలతో చిన్న పత్రము తయారు చేసి ఇచ్చినాను. ఆ కరపత్రాన్ని అచ్చు వేయించి పంచినాను. కొద్దిమంది మాత్రమే శ్రద్ధగా తీసుకొన్నారు. చదివిన వారెందరో తెలియదు. సాహితీ సదస్సు మాతాపితరుల జ్ఞాపకానికి అవకాశమిస్తుందని ఆ సంఘ అధ్యక్షులు శ్రీ చంద్రశేఖర కల్కూర గారు తెలియజేసినప్పుడు మా తండ్రి గురించి మరికొంత అధీకృత సమాచారం సేకరించడానికి ప్రయత్నించినాను.

శ్రీ సి. నారాయణస్వామి ఎల్.ఐ.సి. విశ్రాంత అధికారి వద్ద "భారతదేశ గ్రంథాలయాలు పుస్తక ప్రచారకులు, పుస్తకవిక్రయదారులు" అనే ఆంగ్ల పుస్తకము ఆంధ్ర గ్రంథాలయము నుండి సేకరించినదే ఇచ్చినాడు. మరికొంత అధీకృత సమారం గురించి విజయవాడ సర్వోత్తమ గ్రంథాలయముకు వెళ్ళినపుడు అక్కడి సెక్రటరి శ్రీమతి రావి శారద గారు, లైబ్రేరియన్ శ్రీ శివరామకృష్ణయ్య గారు, వేటపాలెం వెళ్ళినపుడు సరస్వతి నిలయము అధ్యక్షులు శ్రీ మల్లికార్జునరావు గారు గ్రంథాలయ సిబ్బంది మరికొంత సమాచారం అందించినారు.

విశ్రాంత సంచాలకులు, కార్యదర్శి, జిల్లా గ్రంథాలయ సంస్థ శ్రీ వెలగా వెంకటప్పయ్య గారు మీ తండ్రి మరణించి 40 సంవత్సరములవుతుంది. వారిని గురించి ఒక పుస్తకము తయారు చేయమని ఉత్సాహపర్చినారు. ప్రతి దినము తెలుగులో 20 పుస్తకములు విడుదల అవుతున్నాయి. టి.వి. మరియు సినిమా ప్రభావాల వల్ల ఈ కాలం పుస్తకం చదివే వాళ్ళే కరువైనారు. గ్రంథాలయాల అవసరాలు ఆన్‌లైన్ లో దొరికే సమాచారం వల్ల తగ్గిపోయింది అనే నిర్వేదం ఉండింది. ఆన్‌లైన్‌లో వ్యక్తుల సమాచారం పొందు పరిచే అవకాశం కూడా వుంది.

స్వాతంత్ర్యానికి పూర్వం 24 సంవత్సరాలు ఆ తరువాత గ్రంథాలయాల అవసరం సామాన్య ప్రజలకు ఎక్కువగా వున్న దినాలలో 25 సంవత్సరాలు సేవలు అందించిన (1923-1972) ఆంధ్ర గ్రంథాలయము స్థాపించి నిర్వహించిన కీ॥శే॥ శ్రీ ముచ్చుకోట వెంకటరామయ్యగారి ఆశయం పూర్తయిందనే భావించి వారి గురించి తెలియజేయాలన్న తపనతో ఈ పుస్తక రూపకల్పనకు పూనుకున్నాను.

చాలామంది భూములేమయినాయి అని ప్రశ్న వేస్తున్నారు. చాలా కాలంగా సాగు చేస్తున్న వారికే వ్రాసి ఇచ్చి వారు ఇవ్వగలిగిన పైకంతో గ్రంథాలయం గురించి చేసిన అప్పులు కొంతవరకు తీర్చబడ్డాయి. ప్రభుత్వమైనా రకరకాల మాన్యాలను అలాగే సాగుచేసేవారికి ఇచ్చేస్తున్నది.

ద్వంద్వార్థాల సమాహారం జీవితం. మా ముత్తాత గారు నమ్మినది శివరామ భక్తి. మా తాత గారు నమ్మినది ఆడంబరము లేని జీవితము, కరణంగానైనా ఏమీ ఆశించకుండా చెయ్యగలిగిన సహాయం చెయ్యడం మానాన్న గారు నమ్మినది **"సర్వజన సేవ్యమే యొకసేవమని అట్టిసేవనమే భగవత్ సేవనమని"**.

నాకు ఆస్తులు పూర్తిగా కరిగిన తరువాత కుటుంబ పోషణ, పిల్లలకు దారి చూపడం ముఖ్యమైన సేవ అని నాకు అనిపించింది. ఏది ఏమైనా ఆంధ్రగ్రంథాలయము మూతపడడము బాధాకరము.

ఏ వ్యక్తీ, కుటుంబానికి, పదవికి, సమాజానికి, ప్రకృతికి, సముచితంగా న్యాయం చేసేదానికి వీలుపడదు అన్నది భరతవాక్యం.

యుగ అవసరాలనుసారం మహాత్ములు జన్మిస్తారు. భగవంతుడు వారికి కావలసిన విభూతులను అనుగ్రహిస్తాడు. చాలా మంది మహనీయుల పిల్లలు వారి తల్లిదండ్రులతో పోలిస్తే సూర్యుని ముందు దివిటీల మాదిరి ఉండడం సహజం.

ఇటీవల వారు స్వాతంత్ర్య సమరయోధులు శ్రీ డా॥ రాజేంద్రప్రసాద్, శ్రీ వల్లభాయ్ పటేల్, లాల్ బహద్దూర్ శాస్త్రి, నీలం సంజీవరెడ్డి గార్ల పుత్రులను గురించి **CNN, IBN** టీ.వి. ఛానల్ వారు ప్రసారం చేసినారు. మహనీయుల పిల్లలు సాదాసీదా జీవనము చేస్తూ. రాజకీయాలకు సమాజసేవకు దూరంగా జీవనము సాగిస్తున్నారు.

సక్రము కర్మ చేయడం ప్రాణి బాధ్యత. ఫలితం దైవానుగ్రహం.

స్వాతంత్ర్యం కోసం అనేక రకాల ఉద్యమాలు జరిగాయి.
గుర్తింపు పొందని కార్యకర్తలకు వారి కుటుంబాలకు
ఘన నివాళులులర్పిస్తునాను...

ముచ్చుకోట వేంకట రామయ్య చంద్రశేఖర్,

విశ్రాంత సంయుక్త సంచాలకులు భూగర్భ జల శాఖ,

41-554, కొత్తపేట. కర్నూలు.

Annexure.4

TRANSLATED FROM TELUGU TO ENGLISH

Document No-5 of 1904.

Tadipatri taluk muchukota village, in the house of Ramaiah,Presented on-Year-1904month- june date- 22- daytime 12"o"clock-accepted by karanam Ramaiah that it is as per his wish. Thumb impression-Karanam Ramaiah S/O.Nallappa-brahmin-muchukota.

Supported proof by V.HanumanthaRao S/O.V.SanjeevaRao,Brahmin,Police Inspector,Tadipatri.

Adopted son of Bhattar Venkatanarsu,Venkatarayudu Brahmin- livelihood, karanam,gifts, Muchukota.

Witness signatures,.

Year-1904,month- june, date- 22-K.S.Subbaiah sub registrar-BookIII-volume1-pages 209-210 –registered asNumber-5, 1904 month- june date- 22 Fees remitted-Fourteen Rupees-Signature- K.S.Subbaiah-SEAL.

Year-1904month- June- date- 22-Anantapur district-Tadipatri Taluk –sub Tadipatri,Tadipatri resident Smartha Brahmin,livelihood police inspector Velidindla Hanumantharao"s son Subrahmanyam,

The same taluq,resident of Muchukota village,smartha Brahmin livelihood Karanam gifts , Karanam Venkatrayud"s son Venkataramaiah,

To these two,

Resident of Muchuokota village, Tadipatri taluq, smartha Brahmin livelihood,karanam and gifts, karanam Nallapa's son Karanam Ramaiah gives rights of properties by writing in this will, is as follows: lands and houses included in muchukoa village,in Rayalacheruvu, yadiki, Vemulapadu Konuppalapadu villages of tadipatri taluk tadipatri sub district of Anantapur district,lands and houses in Peravali village of Anantapur taluk,Anantapur district,lands as gifts in the name of Jambisetti Kistappa and in my procession and enjoyment in Burgula village of peyapilli sub district of Pathikonda taluk of Kurnool district,all these in said villages either as pattas or gifts of lands that stand in my name excepting those sold by me either to your father or others, all properties belonging to me, as you are sons of my daughters, after me and my wife lifetime, both of you shall be responsible and with equal rights enjoy the properties. The leases issued by me shall be implemented. The land gifted to my elder daughter Eswaramma during her marriage time S.No.333,acs1.45 tharam Rs.2-14-0 shall be given back to you. The lands gifted for the Rameswaraswamy temple temple in Muchukota village fields with S.Nos.168 acs5-3,tharamRs.10-1-0,S.No.177acs,1.6 tharam Rs.3/4.0.,S.No.14acs.12-14 tharamRs.4-9-0.,those specified in Rayalaceruvu, Yadiki, Vemulapadu, Kamalapadu,Konuppalpadu, pinnepalli villages,burgula village,shall be utilized for conducting rituals as inams and you shall act as managers.You shall be responsible and conduct as specified and enjoy equally after our lifetime. This will is effected by me as per my desire./Agreed by me Karanam Ramayya,witnesses1)Ammalldinne pati Adinarayanappa muchukota Balireddy S/O.Narsireddy .scribe by Patiloni Ravi Kondaiah.

Annexure-5

Translated from telugu to English

Document No.1024 of 1926,filed in book1,Vol 170pages 146,147,Dt.12-7-1926.

Gift of land, house deed.

Gift deed given to resident of Kurnool town,Kurnool District, Manager Andhragranthalayam, upstairs H.No.193

By Kurnool town,Kurnool District resident teacher Muchukota venkataraaiah S/O Karanam VenkataRayudu.

I firmly believe that, "Serving all, is a service, such a service is service to God". So I started above referred library on 1-8-1923, which will facilitate to improve knowledge, Telugu language. I wish that this library should render service permanently as long as Sun, Moon, Stars exists. I wish retain the Management of library as hereditary function, so as please God I handed over the following schedule properties to the Manager of the library. The Manager cannot mortgage or sell the properties. He can utilize the income from properties so as to see that library functions properly, or for its improvement.

This Gift deed is as per my willingness.

Schedule:-

1)Kurnool town,Kurnool District 41 Kothapeta street,No.103 house upstairs,19feet length,13 feet width,east door,all sides 193 no house building.

2)Chinna Kopperla village lands in my procession and enjoyment Kurnool District Koilakuntla sub district, details

S.No	Khushki/ inam	S.No.	Acers/ cents	Tharam Rs.As.Ps.	Name	direction
1.	D	221part	2.43	1-3-6	Chouti chenu1/2	north
2.	D	229part	2.58	5-2-6	Nallavaguchenu1/2	north
3.	D	241part	6.471/4	12-15-3	Chandraiah chenu	north
4.	D	237part	0.971\2	1-15-0	Thirugu gadda1/2	east
5.	D	235part	0.13	0-4-0	Thirugu gadda1/2	east

Note:-,In case,residents in ground floor,item no1 H.No193, feel inconvenience, because of functioning of library in the upstairs, alternate building of not less than value of Rs.500 can be given and this building can be take back by owners.

Witnesses:-12-7-7-1926

M.Venkataramaah teacher,C.M.H.School

BJ.Rackwood princepal,Coles Meorial High School

O.LakshmanaswamyBar at law

Scribed in own handwriting

Bounded by-upstairs H.No.193, In the North Ramoji garden,East pullajirao house,South High road,West Seshaiah house.

Annexure-6

TRANSLATED FROM TELUGU TO ENGLISH

DOCUMENT NO.1262 DT.24-8-1926

Rs.500/ Document of Exchange of properties;-24thday,August month 1926 year; individual1)I,Resident of Kothapeta Kurnool town,Kurnool district,Manager Andhragranthalayam ,individual 2) Resident of same district same taluk, town Venkataramaiah,S/O.Karanam Cenkatarayudu,teacher ,document of exchange of properties between the two.

We are exchanging properties as being described- schedule ,A, belonging to individual 1,manager Andhragranthalayam value Rs.500,toM.Venkataramaiah—described in schedule,B,belonging to individual 2. M.Venkataramaiah valued at Rs.500 to Manager Andhragranthalayam From now onwards individuals shall enjoy the properties they got.

Conditions laid in Gift deed document date: 12-7-1926 and registered as 1024 in sub registrar office shall apply to the property of Andhragranthalayam, in B schedule.

Schedule A property given to Muchukotavenkataraaiah teacher – in Kurnool district Kurnool town No.41, Kothapeta street.House No.193 upstaires 19feet length,13 feet width,east door,193 house in all sides. Bounderies in North Ranoji garden,in the East Pullaji house South high road,West Seshaiah house.

B schedule property given to Andhragranthalayam,-Kurnool district. Kurnool town, Kothapeta Ward No-41 on the center of road trending East West, bounderies-East Sri Venkateswara swamy house,South Venkoji,Abdul Rahiman houses,open spaces,in te western side passage to Venkoji house.

The plot has open space with dimensions,east west12 yards,north south 81/2 yards towards South is 14 yards in east,west,41/2 yards North South.Kurnool Municipality No.278.Entrance has stone chaptas for sittng. The house is sold by Bindukuru Mamillapale,Aswartharammyya garu and his wife Ramalakshmma garu claiming full responsibility and written on 21-2-26 and registered on 9-3-1926 at registrar office Kurnool.

Signed:-M.Venkataramaiah,Manager Andhragranthalayam.

M.Venkataraiah,teacher C M H School

Annexure-7

TRANSLATED FROM TELUGU TO English

Deed No.123 of 1941 Dt.22-1-1941.

Sale deed.Rs 1200.22-1-1941Seller- Muchukota Venkataramaiah S/O Muchukota Venkatarayudu, teacher, Narasimha Raopeta Kurnool,Brahmin by casteaged 45years.

Purchaser-secretary,Andhragranthalayam,Kurnool.

To the above library I donated house in Kothapeta ward No 41-House No 424,is kept vacant as was not useful I hereby cancel the gift and sold the house. In lieu of the house I handed over by sale to Manager Andhragranthalayam the following lands indicated in schedule which is in my procession and enjoyment. From now onwards Manager Andhragranthalayam can utilize the property with all rights for maintenance of library. Either I or my successors will not have any rights so is the sale deed.

Schedule:-

S.No	Khushki /Inam	Survey No.	Acres/ cents	Tharam Rs.As.Ps.	Name	direction
1	D	124	5.84	11.11.0	Half of Rangappachenu	
2	D	153	0.28	0.56	Half of Aremanu chenu	North
3	D	180	5.22	10.7.0	Aremanuchenu	North
4	D	181	0.33	o.10.6	Aremanuchenu	North
5	D	182	1.12	2.40	Aremanuchenu	east
6	D	233/1	2.3	2.9	Thummakulagadda	

M.Venkataramaiah

Annuxure-8

Translated from Telugu to English

Document No.36 of 1941 Dt.1941

Year1941-Januaru7th:-cancellation of house gift ded

Person registering the document,M.VenkataramaiahS/O.Karanam Venkatarayudu, teacher, Narasimharaopeta, teacher,Brahmin,age,44,years.

Previously I donated to Kurnool Andhragranthalayam, house located Kurnool, ward 41 bearing house No.424 cost Rs1000 was not useful for the purpose of library because of reasons noted hereunder, is vacant so I hereby cancel the house gift deed. The gift deed is registered in Registers office in book 1,volume55,page 340 as 24/1926.Reasons-1) I have shifted my residence from Kothepeta to Narasimharaopeta.The library is not convenient to operate either for or my family.2)During the non functioning periods funds are not available to provide a sweeper or watchman3)funds are not available to pay municipality tax and water tax 4A)Children climb wall enter library and play creating nuisance 4B)Narasimharaopeta is better place with wider streets, healthy and pleasant lace,4C)Narasimharaopeta is nearer to schools, student hostels, residences of employees4D)Cildren at times open the taps to drain water which is making the area slushy and creating nuesence5)appointed servants are not attending duty on time or stay till specified time, oil given for lamps is misused 6)Space available is not sufficient for developing library 7)As the house is not being used for residence, being used as dump yard8)Toilet facility is not available so not being chosen for i residential purposes by tenants,9)funds are not available to appoint another exclusive librarian 10)Library working hours are from%to7 in the evening. During winter and rainy season It is difficult reach library as my residence is far away and so I am keeping the library in my house. I am cancelling 41-424house gift deed.Old number 41-354.

Annexure-9

Document 828 of 1942-Dt.11-5-1942

Year1942, Month May,Date 11th. Sale deed executed To Resident of Kurnool, Vaisya by caste, occupation business,Anantha Kondaiah Setty,S/OAnantha Gantaiah Setty,

By Muchukota Venkataramaiah S/O Muchukota venkatarayudu resident of Narasimharaopeta Kurnool,Brahmin by caste, occupation employment, is as follows:-The house constructed in the schedule described below is constructed in the plots purchased by me with my own funds and constructed house,mahadi etc. I have made arrangements to sell, sold the house for Rs.9000.

I am in receipt of the money in the manner detailed:- An amount of Rs.2000/-is given to Anantha Nagannasetty towards clearing of mortgage of the house 43-68,also the house in schedule is mortgaged to Nittore Ramaswamyayya and Dr.B Sanjeevarao with a single note and towards clearing the mortgage an amount of Rs.4500 is given by you, Native of Kurnool Badam Krishnaiah filed a suit 113-1941, and compromise settlement is made through court on 22-11-1941and the amount to be paid was Rs.1307/and interest for the amount Rs.37 totaling to Rs.1407 is paid by you.On this day of registration before registrar I am going to be given 1093/ the sum of amounts is Rs.9000 in words rupees nine thousands only is received by me .So the house in schedule is sold and handed over to you. This house is not mortgaged to any other person than Ramaswamyayya and B.Sanjeevarao and is not mortgaged for any other amount except the amount paid by you to clear as specified in this sale deed. I inform that I am selling this house informing that I am only the rightful owner of the house.In case of dispute regarding ownership or title I will clear such disputes with my own funds.I will clear all disputes with my funds ,and bear cost of losses and repaires incurred by you.Further neither I nor any of my successors have any rights on this house. You and your successors can enjoy the property with full rights till Moon shines. I have executed this sale deed with my consent.

Schedule:-Kurnool town, taluk and district situated in Narasimharaopeta plot Nos,19-20 are purchased by me and residential buildings are constructed by me with all rights.old number 43-78,new number 43-91.The house is bounded by-in the East V.Syamasunderarao open space,West road,South conservative street,.Bounded by these form East to West it measures 90feet and from North to South it measures 60 feet. In plot 19 building Is constructed. The rooms included in it.in plot 20 lime trench and rooms South of it etc.In plot 19 are buiding and rooms in it,doors,windows, iron girders, rafters, and electric fittings with bulbs switches,one sealin fan and one table fan,water taps.The house has two main doors in North and another in the South.Full rights exist on the walls in North,West,South and half rights on walls in east.

www.ingramcontent.com/pod-product-compliance
Lightning Source LLC
LaVergne TN
LVHW041114150826
845673LV00007B/2044